The Inner Journey

Marie-Louise von Franz, Honorary Patron

**Studies in Jungian Psychology
by Jungian Analysts**

Daryl Sharp, General Editor

THE INNER JOURNEY
Lectures and Essays
on Jungian Psychology

BARBARA HANNAH
Edited by Dean L. Frantz

Canadian Cataloguing in Publication Data

Barbara Hannah
   The inner journey: lectures and essays on Jungian psychology

(Studies in Jungian psychology by Jungian analysts; 88)

Includes bibliographical references and index.

ISBN 0-919123-89-9

1. Jungian psychology.
I. Frantz, Dean L.   II. Title.   III. Series.

BF173.J85H326 2000   150.19'54   C99-931699-0

INNER CITY BOOKS
Box 1271, Station Q
Toronto, ON M4T 2P4, Canada

Telephone (416) 927-0355 / Fax (416) 924-1814
E-mail: icb@inforamp.net / Web site: www.inforamp.net/~icb

Honorary Patron: Marie-Louise von Franz.
Publisher and General Editor: Daryl Sharp.
Senior Editor: Victoria Cowan.

INNER CITY BOOKS was founded in 1980 to promote the
understanding and practical application of the work of C.G. Jung.

Cover: "Lotus Mandala," monoprint by Vicki Cowan, © 1999.

Printed and bound in Canada by University of Toronto Press Incorporated

CONTENTS

See final pages for descriptions of other Inner City Books

Left to right: Barbara Hannah, M. Esther Harding, Marie-Louise von Franz
(about 1960)

Preface
by Dean L. Frantz

Barbara Hannah is one of those people who was active during the golden years of Jungian psychology. Among her best-known colleagues were M. Esther Harding, Irene Claremont de Castillejo, Eleanor Bertine, Emma Jung and Marie-Louise von Franz, all "classical" Jungians, by which I mean they took Jung's message to heart and amplified it according to their own experience.

The lectures and essays in this book are part of Hannah's continuing legacy to future generations. They are a window through which we can see into the mind of this remarkable woman who never failed to give Jung and his psychology the credit for her own individuation.

Some interesting responses have been shared with me following the publication in 1992 of Hannah's *Cat, Dog and Horse Lectures and "The Beyond,"* along with a biographical sketch of the woman who was my mentor during my years of training in Zurich.

Readers of that book realize what a tremendous debt I owe to Miss Hannah, as she was generally known. She will always have my undying gratitude for sharing with me her wisdom, insights and total commitment to the unconscious. Many people told me of their appreciation for her writings which had not previously appeared in print. They were also grateful for a glimpse into the life of this wise old woman, who knew Jung as both student and colleague for three decades. She was extremely modest about her achievements and her life, reticent to reveal details of her own journey toward wholeness, so information about her is minimal. In one sense, it could be said that she lived in the shadow of Jung.

Some of the people who were Miss Hannah's analysands, or who shared common experiences with her, have been gracious enough to record their thoughts. There is space in the Appendix here for only a few of these memories, but enough to make it clear that her influence on the lives of those whom she touched continues to this day.

Foreword
by Marion Woodman

Season of mists and mellow fruitfulness,
Close bosom-friend of the maturing sun;
Conspiring with him how to load and bless
With fruit the vines that round the thatch-eaves run.
—John Keats, "To Autumn."

This ode by Keats echoed through my thoughts like an old friend as I walked for the first time to the C.G. Jung Institute on Gemeindestrasse in Zurich. It was the fall of 1974. I had landed at the airport at 8 a.m. and was stunned by jet lag. Further stunned by being addressed in German, I managed to register at the front desk and then sought refuge in the library.

"What madness possessed me to come here?" I asked myself. Then a book with a bright yellow jacket almost leaped off the bookshelf. It was *Striving Toward Wholeness* by Barbara Hannah. I suddenly realized it was about the Brontës, and about their problems as P.K.'s (Preacher's Kids). Within half an hour, I knew that the author of that book was the right analyst for me. When I asked for Miss Hannah's phone number, I was assured that she was a very old lady, certainly not taking any new analysands. So I wrote her a note thanking her for the unique insights her book had opened to me.

The next afternoon the phone rang. It was Miss Hannah inviting me to tea. Over our cups she said: "You are a parson's daughter; I am a parson's daughter. When I came to Zurich, Jung told me that only a parson's child could handle a parson's child." And so, with eighty-one years of experience attempting to integrate the intensity of the opposites in a child of the manse, she took me on.

For me, one session highlights the essence of our work together. Fiercely independent and well aware of the conflicts that analysis would entail, I was financing myself in Zurich with my own money saved over a twenty-five year teaching career. I was left somewhat stranded when the dollar dropped in ratio to the Swiss franc, and I found myself needing money for values that were of utmost importance to me, but values of which I knew my husband would not approve. Since he was my sole other financial resource, I was in an intolerable conflict.

In an analytic session, I said, "My husband wouldn't give me money for that purpose."

"Then lie to him," Miss Hannah said.

"But, Miss Hannah," I said, aghast at her response, "that would not be honest."

"My dear," she said, looking me straight in the eye, "we're not talking about honesty, we're talking about getting along with men."

The words resonated in my being—as the right words spoken in the right moment always do. I knew the words were coming from the Self. I knew they had nothing to do with taking revenge on men, nothing to do with manipulating men for my own insidious purposes. Exactly what they did mean, I did not know, but they rang true.

As I left Lindenbergstrasse 15, where Miss Hannah lived and practiced (in the same house as Marie-Louise von Franz), consciousness began to dawn. Someone was going to be betrayed in the situation, either my husband who had no way of comprehending the feeling values involved, or myself who had pondered their worth for weeks. What was of utmost value to me as a woman would, I thought, seem foolish, hair-brained, stupid to him. I began thinking back through my life to the countless times I had betrayed my own feeling values and accepted some man's logical, rational decision that left me saying, "Yes, it is for the best," while at the same time feeling dead inside. Remembering the many times I had withdrawn from a fight, gone ahead and done what I wanted to do alone, leaving the man to do what he wanted to do alone, I realized how the betrayal of my own feeling betrayed his as well. I realized how failure to be true to myself resulted in being false to others.

That night I wrote a detailed, honest letter to my husband. He replied with feeling and with money. That immediacy, that presence, that feminine capacity to live the moment as it presents itself, is my most precious gift from Miss Hannah. Her own trust in the Self made that gift possible.

Knowing her in the autumn of her life, I saw the full flowering of her sense of humor, her forthrightness and her love. Never sentimental about herself or others, she constantly dealt with the opposites within the Self with unflinching courage. She knew when to use her masculine side to discern what was irrelevant and what was essential, and when to rely on her feminine side to receive what the Self was ready to give. Her surrender to the Self sustained her immense energy, physically and spiritually.

Miss Hannah was my living example of one who lives forever true to the process, holding firm to the opposites until the transcendent emerges. And while I have seen her faith stumble in the fires of adversity, I have also seen her steady herself and stand firm in the flames—burning until the dross was burned to silver and gold. Her commitment, which was at the same time her detachment, made me understand the love that Wordsworth writes about, a love that makes

> *. . . a thing endurable, which else*
> *Would overset the brain, or break the heart.*[1]

---

[1] "Michael," lines 449f.

Introduction
Barbara Hannah in Perspective
by Vernon Brooks

Address delivered at the Memorial Service, September 12, 1986,
Reformed Church, Küsnacht, Switzerland.

In 1968 Barbara Hannah went to America, to an island off the coast of Maine, to take part in the eightieth birthday celebrations for her old friend and colleague, Esther Harding. She chose "The Beyond" as the subject of a paper which she read there. As she commented at the time, she had dreamed two years earlier that she must "write down all I know about the life beyond death." And after that initial paper on the subject, Miss Hannah continued to maintain her interest in what she referred to as "the subject that grows on one more and more in old age."

Since the first glimmer of consciousness humanity has speculated about physical death and what lies beyond it, from the earliest vague notions of prehistory, through the Christian belief in the resurrection of the body, to recent investigations of contemporary medical scientists. Modern psychology, especially the analytical psychology of C.G. Jung, has also concerned itself with this mysterious area of our existence, and Barbara Hannah was in close touch with those findings, especially the work of Marie-Louise von Franz, her close friend of many years. Whatever the truth about the Beyond may be, she knows more about it today than those of us who remain behind. Miss Hannah was Anglican by birth and Jungian by choice; the idea of resurrection is common to both, as a psychic reality for Jungians, and as an orthodox belief of Christians.

More immediate, in this moment of time-space, however, is what Barbara Hannah represented for us, what she was as a human being, what her influences were during the days of her earthly lifetime. And here we need not speculate. We know.

Dr. Jung once remarked in a seminar that each of us ought to leave some trace in this world that we have been here, that we made a difference. Miss Hannah's traces are manifest and manifold.

There are, first of all, the published writings, small in number but looming large in their significance. They include a masterpiece, her definitive account of Jung's life and work, which she called a "biographical memoir." It is an honest, clear-eyed, deeply-felt book, which will remain invaluable as source material for any future biography which cares to go beyond the superficial events of Jung's life. Her studies on the individuation process, published under the title *Striving Toward Wholeness,* and on active imagination will also remain seminal works on both subjects.

No less unforgettable to those of us who were present are our memories of the lectures she gave over many years, mostly at the Jung Institute here, but also at other institutes and clubs throughout the Jungian world. Many of these lectures are preserved on tape, where not only her shrewd comments on the human condition are in evidence, but also the inimitable manner in which they were delivered. To hear Miss Hannah address an audience was to be acutely aware of a highly individual human being who spoke directly out of her own experience with her own unique verbal fireworks.

Psychic traces of something having happened while Barbara Hannah lived among us may be less materially tangible, but are even more impressive than are the artifacts.

First of all, I think we must recognize her absolute integrity. This was not just a gift from heaven, but was an achievement which came after years of struggle, both inner and outer, the kind of subjective struggle in which the ego abdicates in favor of the Self. This is psychological language, of course, but, as Barbara points out in "The Beyond," it is the equivalent of what Meister Eckhart meant when he said that "if we can only give up our own ego way entirely, God will replace it completely by his will." This is an achievement of the utmost meaningfulness, and Miss Hannah's expression of it was most impressive in her later years, giving her that remarkable aura of authenticity.

Such integrity is only possible for someone who has recognized the relationship between the finite and the infinite, and has found a precarious balance between them where one is able to sustain the awful tension between opposing powers. And it is the rare ability to do this that places Miss Hannah among the more influential of modern spirits. Hers was an influence which expressed itself not in events reported in the daily press, but subterraneously throughout the collective life of mankind. Jung remarked that any hope that the world may escape future destruction depends on how many of us can sustain the tension of opposites within ourselves.

For only in this way can the polarized conflict between political and social opposites be alleviated. If the world were inhabited by a sufficient number of individuals like Barbara Hannah who have managed to achieve this precious but terrible equilibrium, then we might be freed of the apocalypse which hangs over us today. We owe our undying gratitude to all those who are able to do this—as we are therefore deeply indebted to Barbara Hannah.

Closely related to her integrity was her extraordinary feeling function, which prompted a close friend to remark that she was the wisest human being he knew. He did not mean that she was the wisest in the intellectual or academic sense, but that she was wise with the wisdom of the heart. This wisdom was most eloquently expressed in her willing recognition of the role which feeling played in any human situation or relationship. Miss Hannah's own feelings were forthright, never suppressed. They lived their appointed life, and if you were present you knew it. She was afraid of no one, neither of policemen, nor of politicians, nor of officious busybodies, nor of heads of institutions. Her feeling guided her freely and surely among those who came her way; it was pure, uncontaminated, and its purity was a source of strength which supported all of us who walked anywhere near her commanding presence.

Barbara Hannah wrote, in "The Beyond," that "it is the task of life to prepare itself for death—in the sense of creating a condition that represents a detachment from the finite in favor of the infinite."[2] In her final years she gave us an extraordinary example of someone preparing for death. She became a reflection of that "living spirit" which Jung speaks of at the end of his paper on "Psychotherapists or the Clergy":

> The living spirit grows and even outgrows its earlier forms of expression; it freely chooses the men who proclaim it and in whom it lives. This living spirit is eternally renewed and pursues its goal in manifold and inconceivable ways throughout the history of mankind. Measured against it, the names and forms which men have given it mean very little; they are only the changing leaves and blossoms on the stem of the eternal tree.[3]

Barbara Hannah was a carrier of that "living spirit." And because she was, she is assured a renewal in eternity. She has now gone into that Be-

---

[2] *The Cat, Dog and Horse Lectures, and the Beyond,* p. 51.
[3] *Psychology and Religion,* CW 11, par. 538. [CW refers throughout to *The Collected Works of C.G. Jung.*—Ed.]

yond which intrigued her so much, and where the spirit which has left us with so many traces of its reality may find its release from the crosses of mundane life, for it has now detached itself from the finite in favor of the infinite.

Nothing has been said so far about Miss Hannah's professional life. She was one of those who did her training with Dr. Jung, and there does seem to be something special about those analysts, whose number diminishes as the years pass. Those of us who came too late to have analyzed or studied with Jung at least still have an occasional opportunity to work with one of his students and friends.

It was my privilege to have had Barbara Hannah as a personal analyst, and as a friend, for the last eight years. She worked right through to the end. I had my last hour with her two weeks ago today, and would have had another a week ago if she had not left us the day before.

Today we say farewell to a first-rate analyst, a beloved friend and a remarkable human being.

1
Some Glimpses of the Individuation Process
in Jung Himself

Each year on June 6, a memorial service in honor of Jung is held at the C.G. Jung Institute in Küsnacht, Switzerland. At this time the John Freeman BBC interview with Jung, "Face to Face," is shown, and there is a lecture on a topic related to Jungian psychology. The first lecturer in this series was Barbara Hannah, who spoke on June 6, 1967, six years after the death of Jung.

It is noteworthy that she was chosen to initiate this series, because she was one of those closest to Jung in his lifetime. Her subject was especially appropriate, since the individuation process was the summum bonum *of Jung's approach to life.*

In the first half of my life, when I was still drawing and painting, I never could make myself specialize—as most of my artist friends said would greatly improve my technique—because there was some elusive quality that was the only thing I cared to try to either draw or paint. This quality appeared in the most diverse things: sometimes in a landscape, in the roots of a tree, in flowers or in the most banal things, such as a pot or a pan. It also appeared in human beings, but I noticed more and more that it wasn't evident in human beings who were much influenced by modern civilization. It very often appeared in peasants; in South Africa I saw it frequently in the natives; it was sometimes present strongly in very young children and most often of all in animals. I first realized how its presence was quite unpredictable when I was doing some studies of butterflies' wings in the London South Kensington Museum. I would be given a whole drawerful of specimens of the same species and superficially they looked exactly alike, yet I soon realized that only one, or at most two specimens in the whole collection had the quality of which I was in search.

I could not have named this quality. When asked why I was so apparently arbitrary in what I would or would not attempt to reproduce, I felt embarrassed to answer, and stuttered something about complete naturalness or sometimes about perfect specimens, but I knew the latter was incorrect because—in my butterfly experience—I had sometimes found this quality in specimens that had been damaged in preservation, whereas it would be lacking in the next one, which was without the slightest blemish.

Early in my analysis, a dream at last named this elusive quality as *wholeness,* which immediately made sense to me, and put my early blind and unconscious search into focus for the first time. In January 1929, a year or two before this clarifying dream, I had had my first interview with Dr. Jung. Immediately I was struck by the overwhelming presence of this quality, and thought to myself: "This man is as natural as any peasant and yet he also has the most remarkable mind I ever met. I did not know that such a combination was possible, in fact I have always sworn it was not." Of course I did not know on that day, now nearly forty years ago, that Dr. Jung was consciously making a scientific study of that quality of complete naturalness or wholeness which—through my drawing and painting—I had blindly sensed in its original, unconscious form, or possibly had projected into certain things that had a hook ready to receive this projection.

As you all know, as Jung went on with his studies in this field, he named this quality of wholeness "the process of individuation." He found it first in his own confrontation with the unconscious, which is so vividly described in *Memories, Dreams, Reflections,* and then more and more in his work with his patients, but he still felt very lonely in what seemed to him a very strange realm. In fact at times it seemed worse than strange, as he realized how like the material was to what he had already observed in the dreams and fantasies of the insane. He once described to me the dark *nigredo* he went through at that time and the indescribable relief when he found the same images in the writings of the old Gnostics, which was the first field in which he discovered the very same images and symbols. "I felt," he said, "as if I had suddenly found a circle of friends who had shared my experiences and could sympathize with me and understand the whole realm where I had been so lonely and isolated."

Gnostic thought was only the first field where Jung found the symbols of the process of individuation. He learned more and more that if you dig deep enough you find it, as the underlying archetypal pattern, everywhere where man has made a serious and sustained attempt to find the meaning or ultimate value of human existence. It is to be found as the basic foundation of alchemy, every religion, in the rites of primitives, in the remains of all the old lost civilizations all over the world and so on ad infinitum. Or, we can put it differently and say that this basic, archetypal pattern projects itself from the unconscious of every human being who is striving to formulate an impression of the Deity or of the innermost center of their own soul.

I remember vividly how excited I was when I found the same pattern underlying a nineteenth-century novel for which I had long had a great admiration: *Wuthering Heights* by Emily Brontë. (It is to be found in many novels of what Jung calls the visionary type, that is, those that are written from the unconscious and not invented by the conscious of the author. But, as we can tell from her poems, Emily Brontë had an unusually good relation to her creative spirit and thus to the unconscious, so *Wuthering Heights* remains for me by far the most complete example of that I have found up till now.) I was terribly overexcited about this as I wrote my first lecture on the Brontës for the Zurich Psychological Club thirty years ago and, in my enthusiasm, was misguided enough to imagine that Emily Brontë knew what she was doing, that she had *consciously* described the process of individuation!

I need hardly tell you how outraged Dr. Jung was at such a misunderstanding, or how thoroughly I was taught my mistake. As all the end of my first lecture was built upon this fatal error, I was very shattered at the time but—like most fatal mistakes—in the end it taught me much more than if I had just skated around the pitfall. I still remember his words vividly: "There is no such thing as a process of individuation without a conscious individual to live it in themselves; it *is* the individual himself." I murmured that he spoke of it in the alchemists and did they realize it or live it in themselves? (This was before he realized that a few specially gifted alchemists, such as Gerard Dorn, did really know that it was at least connected with themselves but of course this in no way altered the case with Emily Brontë.) "No," he replied, "but even how I speak of the alchemists is very overgenerous, they only describe something totally unconscious to themselves which they really believe that they are seeing in their retorts, and your girl knew even less than they did, and as to your mentioning the Zen masters in connection with her (as, alas, I had been misguided enough to do!) it is inconceivable that you can be so stupid!"

Looking back I can never be sorry that I made such a fool of myself on this occasion, for it upset me so much that for the first time I had to deal with this matter from every aspect or function I could reach. Slowly it became more and more clear to me that the really convincing thing to me down here was not the books that I read nor even Dr. Jung's own seminars—marvelous as those were—but he himself, the man Jung. He was, so to speak, the living proof of his own psychology, in fact he *was* his psychology. If this had not been the case, he could never have been who he was or really known himself.

The realization of the importance of self-knowledge did not, of course, begin with Jung. As far as I know Pythagoras (sixth century B.C.) was the first to put it into words, and since then it has been revived from time to time by particularly wise and far-seeing individuals all over the world. Perhaps one of the clearest descriptions of the value of self-knowledge is to be found in the writings of Richard de St. Victor, a Scotsman and one of the most famous and learned monks of the Victorine order in the twelfth century. In his book, "Benjamin minor," he writes:

> The first and fundamental task of the mind, which strives to climb the summit of knowledge, must be to know itself. It is the summit of knowledge to know that one knows oneself completely. The complete knowledge of the reasonable mind is a great and high mountain. It is higher than the peaks of all worldly knowledge, it looks down from above on all the wisdom of the world and on all the knowledge in the world.[4]

Richard de St. Victor continues by pointing out the weakness of philosophy in this respect:

> What has Aristotle found of this kind, what has Plato found, what of such things has the great multitude of the philosophers found? Verily and without doubt, if they had been able to climb this mountain of their penetrating mind, their effort would have sufficed to find themselves; had they known themselves perfectly, they would never have paid homage to idols, they would never have inclined to the hill of things created, they would never have lifted their head against the creator. Here the searchers failed in the search. Here, they did fail, and therefore it is impossible for them to climb the mountain. "Man lifts himself on high in his innermost and God is uplifted." (Ps. 63 [Vulgate, 63, 7]) Learn to meditate, O man, learn to meditate on thyself, and thou wilt ascend in thine innermost. The more thou improvest daily in self knowledge, the more thou wilt climb above thyself. He who reaches perfect self-knowledge, has already reached the top of the mountain.[5]

---

[4] Quoted by Jung in "Alchemy: The Process of Individuation—Notes on Lectures Given at the Eidgenössische Technische Hochschule, Zürich, 1940-41," p. 23.
[5] Ibid.

Anyone who knew Dr. Jung well will have realized that it was just this knowing himself that made him what he was. There are no fake idols in his psychology; the whole thing is genuine through and through and is— in my experience at least—the one thing that never disappointed me.

Naturally the mountain of self-knowledge that Richard de St. Victor praises so highly here is not mere ego knowledge, not just personal psychology, as Richard makes very clear when he quotes the passage: "Man lifts himself on high in his innermost and God is uplifted." In medieval Christian language, Richard is saying the same thing here as Jung said seven hundred years later:

> As to this self knowledge, this real penetrating knowledge of our own being, do not make the mistake of thinking that it means seeing through the ego. To understand the ego is child's play, but to see through the Self is something totally different. The real difficulty lies in recognising the unknown. No one need remain ignorant of the fact that he is striving for power, that he wants to become very rich, that he would be a tyrant if he had the chance, that he is pleasure seeking, envious of other people, and so on. Everyone *can* know such things of him or herself, because they are mere ego knowledge. But Self knowledge is something completely different, it is learning to know of the things which are unknown.[6]

It was in recognizing the unknown in himself that Jung most excelled and where he laid the foundation for his whole psychology. I think Richard de St. Victor would have said that he reached the "top of the mountain" as few, if any, had done before him. Nor would Richard have accused him of inclining "to the hill of things created" or of "lifting up his head against the creator," as he does not scruple to accuse the philosophers of doing, even Aristotle and Plato. This is all the more remarkable when we remember that Jung grew up in the last quarter of the nineteenth century when the whole spirit of the age was turning more and more toward materialism. In spite of their great merits in the field of personal psychology, both Freud and Adler succumbed to this trend and were unable to see beyond the material and personal. So it must have been particularly difficult for Jung to swim directly against the current of his time and never "incline to the hills of things created." And, as you know, the spirit of the time was also dead against the value of the individual, and more and more tended toward sinking the individual in the mass. Even in the countries where some rights

---

[6] Ibid., p. 72.

were still left to the individual, all introspection or self-examination was dismissed as morbid. Yet Jung never wavered but remained faithful all his life to "climbing the mountain of self knowledge" and thus, as Richard says, not only saw all the wisdom and knowledge of the world spread out before him but saw far beyond there to the eternal in us or, in his own language, to the Self.

But climbing the mountain of self-knowledge, and above all getting a clear objective view of the Self, always entails having it out with the opposites. It is easy enough to accept these intellectually and to talk of the really scalding hot pair of opposites—good and evil—as if they were dark and light, hot and cold, or any other natural pair of opposites. But Jung was a parson's son and I am sure you all remember his description of the agony he went through, already as a schoolboy, when on a day of "radiant sunshine" he thought of God sitting on a golden throne in the blue sky above Basel Cathedral and was suddenly brought up short by a "great hole in his thoughts and a choking sensation" and knew that to think the thought to the end meant "committing the most frightful of sins." He could not sleep for two nights and the days were "sheer torture," which shows us clearly the burning problem that evil was, even then, to Jung. After an agony of indecision, on the third night, he decided to risk thinking the thought to the end and to let the result show him whether he had understood God's will correctly or not. To his intense relief his—by all traditional standards—highly blasphemous thought proved indeed to have been what was asked from him and, instead of "the expected damnation," grace and unutterable bliss descended on him and made him weep "for happiness and gratitude."[7]

I remind you of this early experience of Jung's—although I am sure you already know it—because I think it shows as nothing else can the agonizing problem which the opposites of good and evil represented all his life to Jung. Some seventy years later in his autobiography, in the chapter "Late Thoughts," Jung wrote on the same subject:

> Light is followed by shadow, the other side of the Creator. This development reached its peak in the 20th century. The Christian world is now truly confronted by the principle of evil, by naked injustice, tyranny, lies, slavery, and coercion of conscience. This manifestation of naked evil has assumed apparently permanent form in the Russian nation; but

---

[7] *Memories, Dreams, Reflections,* p. 40.

its first violent eruption came in Germany. That outpouring of evil revealed to what extent Christianity has been undermined in the twentieth century. In the face of that, evil can no longer be minimized by the euphemism of the *privatio boni.* Evil has become a determinant reality. It can no longer be dismissed from the world by a circumlocution. We must learn how to handle it, since it is here to stay. How we can live with it without terrible consequences cannot for the present be conceived.[8]

When one thinks of the state of the world and of evil as a collective problem, it can still in no way be conceived how we can live with it and survive. But—as Jung emphasized again and again—it is only in the individual that any important problem can be solved and—in his own individual psychology—Jung certainly did find a way to live with the dark side of himself and with that of the Creator. He once told me that the experience of God and the Basel cathedral had been the guiding line of his whole life. He realized then once and for all that God at times demands evil of us and that then we must obey whatever it costs us. To do evil—or good either for that matter—lightly, without making the utmost efforts to ascertain the *kairos,* what belongs to the moment, is indeed purely destructive, but to do evil consciously—as Jung thought that blasphemous thought to the end—can be purely creative.

I must own, however, that it took me twenty years to realize that Jung had done more for me with his dark side than with his light. Before then I wasted a terrible lot of time thinking I had been unjustly treated, with foolish, childish jealousy and the like. Then something happened which proved it to me beyond all doubt, and when I told Jung of this experience, he replied that he knew it was true but that it was still very painful to him. He gave the example of the Psychological Club, where he still went to the lectures in those days, and said: "Very often I find myself being really nasty to someone at the Club, saying something cutting or barely greeting them. Then I go home feeling bad about it, knowing I have hurt them and that they will have a bad weekend. And yet—when that person comes next to analysis and I hear their dream—I find that I have said exactly what they needed and that it would have done them great harm if I had indulged myself in being nice to them."

Jung, albeit very painfully, did live with the opposites in himself and, as a result, they became more and more relative to each other and lost their

---

[8] Ibid., pp. 328f.

absolute character. He was also always concerned that his pupils should not just copy him, but learn their own way of dealing with this problem. When people complained to him—as they often did—that the Institute was no haven of peace, he would often reply: "Do you think I have founded a kindergarten where the students find only benevolent fathers and good mothers and where they don't even learn to put a spoon into their own mouth? No, indeed, they must meet the opposites in the Institute during their training and then perhaps they will be able to deal with them in the world later, otherwise there would not be even a remote chance for them."

The opposites certainly do clash against each other in the Institute but it is a great comfort, to me at any rate, that Jung foresaw this and even wanted it to happen in order to increase consciousness in both faculty and students. But it will only do this if we all do our utmost to remember the *kairos* and to ascertain which opposite is being asked of us in each moment. If, on the other hand, we just drift along, allowing first one opposite and then the other to use us, it must end destructively, at all events for ourselves. But if, like Jung, we all suffer the utmost in our choice, then it will end constructively and creatively, and Jung's intention will have been fulfilled.

It is six years today since Jung died. Jung says himself in *Memories:*

> Death is indeed a fearful piece of brutality; there is no sense pretending otherwise. It is brutal not only as a physical event, but far more psychically: a human being is torn away from us, and what remains is the icy stillness of death.[9]

It is so indeed in the great majority of cases, and so far as the warm, genial physical presence of Jung is concerned, it is also true in his own case. What would most of us not give for half an hour's talk with him in the Seestrasse or at Bollingen? But, in another sense, I at all events have found it is less of an icy barrier with Jung than it has been in the great majority of deaths that have affected me closely. And this, I think, is because he still appears in the dreams of many people, and occasionally in their active imagination, almost exactly as he did when he was alive. Very often this gives us the sense of his near presence. But, as he himself also said in the same chapter, we cannot possibly know whether the figure we contact in such cases is "identical with the dead person" or whether it is "a

---

[9] Ibid., p. 314.

psychic projection."[10] Personally I do not feel it matters so very much whether this helpful presence—that usually seems to intervene when there is a problem that is really beyond the strength or knowledge of the dreamer—is the individual Jung or whether it is an archetype that has been brought so much further into consciousness by him through his life that it now more often appears in his form or speaks with his voice.

At all events it is yet one more incentive to do all we can to remain in touch with the unconscious, with the opposites. As Jung says:

> The decisive question for man is: Is he related to something infinite or not? That is the telling question of his life. Only if we know that the thing which truly matters is the infinite can we avoid fixing our interest upon futilities.[11]

These days—when we cannot take up a newspaper without reading of some place where a war may set the world on fire at any moment—are indeed not times when we can afford to ignore such a warning. Relating to the unconscious is and remains our one hope of finding a way that can give us enough support and wisdom to face the outer world, without getting lost in its outer threats. As most of you already know, Jung even went so far as to say that the best chance of the atom bomb not being used was if enough people could stand the tension of the opposites in themselves. And such an attitude may even perhaps give us a chance to answer the "telling question" of our lives in the affirmative.

---

[10] Ibid., p. 301.
[11] Ibid., p. 325.

2
On Active Imagination

This talk was given in Zurich on September 25, 1967, at a Special Lecture Series for the C.G. Jung Educational Center of Houston, Texas.

Part One

As you all know, active imagination—although it differs from its predecessors in being more empirical and scientific in character—is by no means a modern practice. One could even say that it is as old as the earliest efforts of humanity to relate to eternal forces. As soon as we try to open negotiations with such powers, with the idea of coming to terms with them, we instinctively discover some form of active imagination. For instance, if you read the Old Testament attentively from that point of view you will find it is full of such attempts. I only remind you, as one example among a multitude, of the way Jacob shaped his whole course on what he heard the Lord say to him. It is true that, in Jacob's case, the will of the Lord was often revealed in dreams, but by no means always, and Jacob no doubt had inherited a faculty to hear what these forces said to him—whether they are named God or the unconscious makes no essential difference—from his mother Rebecca. It was she who went to "inquire of the Lord" when the twins struggled in her womb, and shaped the whole of her rather dubious methods in dealing with her old husband and her sons on His reply. Rather dubious methods they certainly were, if we judge them from the standpoint of conventional morality, but if we consider that she was carrying out the Lord's will, they take on a very different character.

Rebecca's way of dealing with the puzzle set her by those twins struggling in her womb contains our main motive in still turning to active imagination today. She could not understand what was happening to her and, as Dr. Jung has often said, the only unbearable suffering is suffering we do not understand. So Rebecca asked herself: "If it be so, why am I thus?" and went "to inquire of the Lord." (Gen. 25:22) In principle this procedure was exactly the same as ours. When we experience something as unbearable, or even when the meaninglessness of our life in itself becomes more than we can stand, we turn to a source of greater wisdom in order to increase our understanding.

24

Now, in the days of Jacob and Rebecca, man was still naive and simple enough to go straight to what he then knew to be the fountainhead of knowledge, in the case of the early Jews "the Lord." They just asked what they wanted to know and were still able to hear the reply. There are people who still have this naive simplicity, this certainty concerning their invisible vis-à-vis, but I must say that they are very rare and seem to be becoming, alas, almost extinct. It follows the principle of the Elgoni primitives in East Africa who used to trust their whole fate to the dreams their medicine men had. But they told Jung in 1925, sadly, that since the English came they did not have any more big dreams, for you see the District Commissioner knew what they should do.[12]

Whether we know it or not, more and more in these rational days we all rely on the "District Commissioner" and all he stands for, and have thus forgotten the superhumanly wise guidance that exists in the unconscious, which Dr. Jung even called "absolute knowledge."[13] Originally, humanity gave a name to this absolute knowledge, calling it "God," "the Lord," the "Buddha mind" and so on.

In the very early days of analysis—mainly just after the parting of the ways between Jung and Freud—Dr. Jung went through "a period of inner uncertainty. . . . It would be no exaggeration to call it a state of disorientation. I felt totally suspended in mid-air, for I had not yet found my own footing."[14] Particularly he felt it was necessary to find a completely new attitude to his patients, for he no longer felt the methods he had used while working in close connection with Freud were either valid or satisfactory: "I resolved for the present not to bring any theoretical premises to bear on them [his patients], but to wait and see what they would tell of their own accord. My aim became to leave things to chance."[15]

Later he saw that very little if anything happens "by chance," so what he really did, already then about 1911, was to trust himself and his patients to the unconscious. Thus he made the discovery that by far the most fruitful way of interpreting dreams was to take their own facts as the basis for their interpretation, since theory of almost any kind only distorts and ob-

---

[12] *Memories, Dreams, Reflections,* p. 265.

[13] "Synchronicity: An Acausal Connecting Principle," *The Structure and Dynamics of the Psyche,* CW 8, par. 931.

[14] *Memories, Dreams, Reflections,* p. 170.

[15] Ibid.

scures their meaning.

This new method worked extraordinarily well with his patients, but Dr. Jung himself still felt that he had not found the firm ground he needed under his feet. He *must* know and understand more of his own inner myth. He had to admit that he himself no longer lived by the Christian myth in which the Western world had lived for the past two thousand years and that, though he had written a long book about myths,[16] he did not yet know his own.

He had several very illuminating dreams at that time, but he says that the dreams could not help him over his "feeling of disorientation," for he did not understand them for many years. So at the time he was forced to search further. You can all read for yourselves the steps—dark and dangerous as they often were—by which he found his own highly empirical path of active imagination. It took him many years, for he was not satisfied with learning to see the images of the unconscious, or even with dealing with them actively in his fantasies. He did not feel at ease until he took "the most important step of all": finding their "place and purpose" in his own actual outer life. This, he says, the most important step in active imagination, is "what we usually neglect to do." Insight into the myth of our unconscious, he continues,

> must be converted into ethical obligation. Not to do so is to fall prey to the power principle and this produces dangerous effects which are destructive not only to others but even to the knower.[17] The images of the unconscious place a great responsibility upon a man. Failure to understand them, or a shirking of ethical responsibility, deprives him of his wholeness and imposes a painful fragmentariness on his life.[18]

I think I have said enough to make it very clear that active imagination is no harmless pastime. It is a very serious step and should never be undertaken lightly. It is true that it is not everybody's fate to face the uncon-

---

[16] See *Symbols of Transformation*, CW 5.

[17] This rather curious word "knower," a literal translation of the more usual German *der Wissende*, here means the one who has experienced insight into the unconscious. A man who has had this most valuable insight and fails to draw conclusions from it regarding its place in his outer life becomes the victim of the power principle, which ultimately endangers himself even more than does his environment.

[18] *Memories, Dreams, Reflections*, p. 193.

scious as completely as Dr. Jung did. Such an exploration is a vocation and should never be undertaken without someone who understands. This is the reason why I have begun this lecture by giving you some idea of the depths to which it may go, and the changes in one's whole life that active imagination may lead to—there is never any guarantee, if we once start on this path, as to where it may lead us. Above all, it should never be undertaken without a firm relationship to someone who will understand, or at least sympathize, for it sometimes leads into such cold and inhuman depths that human companionship is absolutely necessary to prevent us from becoming entirely frozen and lost. But, although it is essential to have a human companion in whom one can confide, the actual active imagination is a very individual and even lonely undertaking. I, for one, could never do active imagination with anyone else in the room—however well I knew them.

There is another warning note I should like to sound from the very beginning because I have met several cases lately where, I own to my surprise, I found it was not generally known. It is that one should never take the figures of living people into one's fantasies. Directly there is any temptation to do this, we should stop and inquire again, *very carefully,* into our motives for the whole undertaking, for it is only too likely that we are regressing into old magical thinking, that is, trying to use the unconscious for personal ends—and not really using it in the only legitimate way: to explore the unknown, in as scientific a way as possible, with the motive of finding our own wholeness.

We come here to the great fundamental difference between using active imagination in the right way or the wrong way. The question is: are we doing it honestly to try to reach and discover our own wholeness, or are we dishonestly using it in an attempt to get our own way? The latter may be successful for a time but sooner or later it always leads to disaster.

If we honestly want to find our own wholeness, to live our individual fate as fully as possible, if we truly want to abolish illusion on principle and find the truth of our own being, however little we like what we find, then there is nothing that can help us so much as active imagination. Ultimately it can also lead to far greater independence, freeing us from analysis or any other outer help, than anything else I know of, but I say ultimately because it is the hardest work I know. Unfortunately things are not so simple and direct as they were in the days of Rebecca, and most of us, if not all, have laboriously to clear away the layers of implicit reliance on the "District Commissioner" and the purely rational security he stands for, before we can simply and trustfully "inquire of the Lord," to use that language, to find our way to the absolute knowledge in our unconscious.

A disciple once asked a learned Rabbi why it was that, whereas God spoke so often in the distant past directly to his people, he never did now? The Rabbi, evidently a very wise man, replied: "Man cannot bend *low* enough now to hear what God says." That is exactly it: we shall only hear what God or the unconscious says by bending very low. Seeing and, to the extent possible, accepting our own shadows, is really a *conditio sine qua non* of hearing that voice, for if we are still indulging ourselves with illusions about who and what we are, we have no chance whatever of being real enough to see the images of the unconscious or to hear its voice. Nature and the unconscious always go straight to the point, which is usually very different from what we expect. We need an unbiased mind that has learned to value the truth above everything in order to register and value what we see and hear.

Therefore I never encourage the people working with me to do active imagination in their early analysis, but do my best to focus their attention on their personal shadow and on their anima and animus until I feel they have gained genuine and sufficient knowledge of both these figures. There are exceptions; a few people are naturally gifted in this respect and then they can find active imagination a great help in learning to know both shadow and animus and can use it legitimately from the beginning of their analysis, but they are very rare.

If active imagination seems to be a way that you can profitably follow, and you are fairly sure your motive is really getting to know more about yourself, realize that it follows the principle of the Chinese rain-maker of Kiau Tchou. I expect most of you know this story already but Dr. Jung, who gave us very little direct advice, once said to me, "Never give a seminar (and not often a lecture) without telling the people this story." He had heard it from the famous Sinologist Richard Wilhelm, and on one of the very last Christmases when he attended the Club dinner, shortly before his death, he told it to us again himself. Now there was certainly no one in the room who did not know the story well, and yet, after he had told it, the whole atmosphere of the party changed and I realized, as never before, why he had urged me to repeat it so often.

The Rain-maker

There was a great drought where Wilhelm lived; for months there had not been a drop of rain and the situation became catastrophic. The Catholics made processions, the Protestants made prayers, and the Chinese burned joss-sticks and shot off guns to frighten away the demons of the drought, but with no result. Finally the Chinese said "We will fetch the rain-maker." And from another province a dried up old man appeared. The only thing he asked for was a quiet little house somewhere, and there he locked himself in for three days. On the fourth day the clouds gathered and there was a great snow-storm at the time of the year when no snow was expected, an unusual amount, and the town was so full of rumors about the wonderful rain-maker that Wilhelm went to ask the man how he did it. In true European fashion he said "They call you the rain-maker, will you tell me how you made the snow?" And the little Chinese said: "I did not make the snow, I am not responsible." "But what have you done these three days?" "Oh, I can explain that. I come from another country where things are in order. Here they are out of order, they are not as they should be by the ordinance of heaven. Therefore the whole country is not in Tao, and I am also not in the natural order of things because I am in a disordered country. So I had to wait for three days until I was back in Tao and then naturally the rain came."[19]

The greatest use of active imagination really is to put us—like the rain-maker—into harmony with ourselves so that the right things may happen around us instead of the wrong. Although perhaps even speaking of the Chinese Tao may seem to impart a rather exotic flavor to what is really a simple matter of everyday experience. We find it in our most colloquial language: "He got out of bed on the wrong side this morning," or as the Swiss say, "with the left foot first." Such expressions aptly express a psychological condition where we are not in harmony with our own unconscious. We are ill-tempered and disagreeable, and it follows, as the night the day, that we have a disintegrating effect on our environment, the exact opposite of the effect which evidently emanated from the rain-maker.

One can see these effects very clearly in the two opposite activities of prayer and black magic. The mystics, as you know, bent their whole endeavor toward achieving union with God or, as we would express it, in going into themselves until the ego was to a great extent replaced by the Self. There are a great many stories of the effects—even described as miraculous—that they had on their environment. For instance, like the rain-

---

[19] *Mysterium Coniunctionis,* CW 14, par. 604, note 211.

maker of Kiau Tchou, St. Gertrude, the Benedictine Abbess, was supposed to be able to influence the weather. There are endless stories of her being able to avert hail by prayer, bring about the cessation of a too severe frost, save the harvest from storm at the last moment, and so on. It is interesting that in her recorded prayer, she emphasizes that she does not wish to impose her ego will on God but would just like to draw His attention to the facts![20] That is, she attempts to produce a complete harmony betweeen herself and God which will not be disturbed whether He answers her prayer or not.

We are not concerned here with whether these effects—natural or miraculous—actually took place, but with the fact that countless people have believed that they did, for this in itself is psychological evidence pointing to a deep-rooted human conviction that harmony with God or the Self has an effect on the environment.

The same is true of the widespread conviction that witches can provoke storms. They were always supposed to do this in connection with the devil or some demon—that is, with a disorderly power. The idea is that they went out of themselves, created a disorder like the ill-temper we have just spoken of, and that this brought about the wrong weather, in exactly the reverse sense to the story of the rain-maker of Kiau Tchou.

Whether the state of one man can actually influence the weather does not concern us either, for it is absolutely impossible to prove one way or the other. I have only given you these examples because they form extreme and visible cases—believed in all times and places by a *consensus gentium*—of the emanations which proceed from a harmonious or disordered relation of individuals to their own unconscious. It is evident that both the *unio mystica* of the saint and the witch's pact with the devil are too one-sided; the one believes in a completely righteous God and dismisses evil more or less as a *privatio boni,* and the other hopes that the devil, the lord of this world, is the more powerful of the two and therefore takes his side, hoping to get more out of him, so to speak. Our task in coming to terms with the unconscious, therefore, is much more difficult than the foregoing examples, for we are obliged to deal with both sides at once. This belongs to the problem of our time.

Both the prayer and contemplation of the mystic and the pact with the

---

[20] From "Life and Revelations of St. Gertrude." [Source unknown.—Ed.]

devil or the witch are closely related in active imagination. That is, both represent an *active* attempt to come to terms with an invisible force, to explore the unknown country of the unconscious. The reason the effect of the mystic is more favorable than that of the witch can be explained psychologically by the fact that the mystic attempts to give up all ego demands, whereas the witch tries to use the forces of the unconscious for his or her ego purposes. In other words, the mystic tries to sacrifice the one-sided ego for the sake of the whole, whereas the witch attempts to use forces which belong to the totality for the sake of the part, the limited conscious ego.

We have all experienced the fact that our conscious intentions are constantly crossed by unknown—or relatively unknown—opponents in the unconscious. Perhaps the simplest definition of active imagination is to say that it gives us the opportunity of opening negotiations with the unconscious, and in time of coming to terms with it. In this it differs from the dream in which we have no control over our own behavior. Of course with the majority of cases in practical analysis the dreams are sufficient to reestablish a balance between conscious and unconscious. It is only in certain cases, which we will go into in more detail later, that more is required. But, before we go further, I owe you a short description of the techniques that can be used.

In every case, the goal is to get in touch with the unconscious and that entails, in some way or other, giving it an opportunity to express itself. (Anyone who is convinced that the unconscious has no life of its own should not even attempt the method.) To give it this opportunity it is nearly always necessary to overcome a greater or lesser degree of conscious cramp in order to allow the fantasies that are always more or less present in the unconscious to come up into consciousness. Dr. Jung once told me that he thought the dream was always going on in the unconscious but that it usually needs sleep and the complete cessation of attention to outer things for it to register in consciousness at all. Therefore, as a rule, the first step in active imagination is to learn to see or hear the dream while we are awake.

Jung says in his commentary on "The Secret of the Golden Flower":

> Each time the fantasy material is to be produced, the activity of consciousness must again be put aside. In most cases the results of these efforts are not very encouraging, at first. They usually consist of webs of

fantasy which yield no clear origin or goal. Also the way of getting at these fantasies is individually different. For many people, it is easiest to write them; others visualize them. In cases of a high degree of conscious cramp, oftentimes the hands alone can fantasy; they model or draw figures that are often quite foreign to the conscious mind. These exercises must be continued until the cramp in the conscious mind is released, in other words, until one can *let things happen,* which was the immediate goal of the exercise. In this way a new attitude is created, an attitude which accepts the non-rational and the incomprehensible simply because it is what is happening. This attitude would be poison for a person who had already been overwhelmed by things that must happen, but it is of the highest value for one who chooses, with an exclusively conscious critique, only the things acceptable to his consciousness from among the things that happen, and thus is gradually drawn out of the stream of life in stagnant backwater.[21]

In other places, Jung includes movement and music among the ways it is possible to reach these fantasies. He points out that with movement—although sometimes of the greatest help in dissolving the cramp of consciousness—the difficulty lies in registering the movements themselves and, if there is no outer record, it is amazing how quickly things that come from the unconscious disappear again from the conscious mind.

As to movement, Jung suggests repetition of the releasing movements until they are really fixed in the memory and, even then, it is my experience that it is as well when possible to put something on paper, either to draw the pattern made by the dance or movement, or to write a few words of description, just so as to prevent it from disappearing altogether in a few days.

In the same commentary, Jung says of the types:

One man will chiefly take what comes to him from without, and the other what comes from within, and, according to the law of life, the one will have to take from the outside something that he never could accept before from outside, and the other will accept from within things which would always have been excluded before. This reversal of one's being means an enlargement, heightening, and enrichment of the personality when the previous values are retained along with the change, provided,

---

[21] Richard Wilhem and C.G. Jung, *The Secret of the Golden Flower: A Chinese Book of Life,* pp. 93f. [For a later translation of this passage, see "Commentary on 'The Secret of the Golden Flower,' " *Alchemical Studies,* CW 13, pars. 21ff.—Ed.]

of course, that these values are not mere illusions. If the values are not retained the individual goes over to the other side, and passes to nonsense and even from rationality to mental disturbance. The way is not without danger. Everything good is costly and the development of personality is one of the most costly of all things. It is a question of saying *yes* to oneself, as the most serious of tasks, of being conscious of everything one does, and keeping it constantly before one's eyes in all its dubious aspects—truly a task that taxes us to the utmost.[22]

As a rule, it takes a very long time—many years usually—before the two sides of the personality, represented by conscious and unconscious, can be brought into Tao, to use this Chinese term again. Although, as I mentioned before, this term may have an exotic sound to Western ears, it is really the most practical of words. Dr. Jung writes:

It is characteristic of the Western mind that it has no concept for Tao. The Chinese character is made up of the character for "head" and that for "going." Wilhelm translates Tao by Sinn (meaning). Others translate it as "way," "providence." or even as "God," as the Jesuits do. . . . "Head" can be taken as consciousness and "to go" as traveling by a way, thus the idea would be: to go consciously or the conscious way.[23]

There is another technique in dealing with the unconscious by means of active imagination which I have always found of the greatest help, namely conversations with contents of the unconscious that appear personified. Dr. Jung used to say that generally this was a later stage in active imagination, and I did not even realize the possibilities until I went to work with Jung himself. It is indeed recommended in his *Two Essays on Analytical Psychology,* and those of you who have read the chapter on "The Confrontation with the Unconscious" in *Memories* will remember that he took to it fairly early in, though not at the beginning of, his own experiments with the method. Also, those of you who have read my case study of "Anna Marjula" will remember that she used painting—the visual rather than the auditory method—for many years and at times combined the two methods very successfully.[24]

The technique for both the visual and the auditory methods consists in being able to let things happen—in the way Dr. Jung described in the pas-

---

[22] Ibid., pp. 94f. *[Alchemical Studies,* CW 13, par. 24.—Ed.]

[23] Ibid., p. 97. *[Alchemical Studies,* CW 13, par. 28.—Ed.]

[24] [See Hannah, *Encounters with the Soul: Active Imagination As Developed by C.G. Jung,* pp. 133ff.—Ed.]

sages quoted above. Then, after taking just enough note of what happened or what was said, one *actively* enters the scene or conversation oneself. If this is not done, fantasizing never becomes active imagination but remains a sort of passive cinema, or one listens, as it were, to a voice on the radio. To be able to do this is necessary but it very soon becomes harmful if indulged in too long. It is a way, par excellence, of having it out with the unconscious (what Jung called an *Auseinandersetzung),* and for that it is necessary to have one's own firm standpoint as well as being able to recognize the point of view of the unconscious.

Part Two

When I gave my first course on active imagination at the Zurich Institute in the spring of 1951, several of the analysts here felt the need to know what I was going to say, since of course many of their analysands come to the Institute seminars. I was therefore asked to give a lecture before the course opened. As a marvelous surprise, at the last moment Dr. Jung himself came to the lecture, with the result that the ensuing discussion was one of the most interesting that I have experienced in my now nearly forty years at the Institute. Frau Aniela Jaffé fortunately was there and took a few shorthand notes of it.

Dr. Jung began the discussion by telling me that I should begin by indicating *when* active imagination was advisable. He confirmed, as I had been emphasizing, that it is by no means always to be undertaken, but only in certain cases, and said I should give my students more detailed instructions. He mentioned six reasons for advising it. I noted these six in my paper "On Active Imagination" which was printed in *Spring 1953,* but I should like to repeat them here with more comment and examples. But before I begin I should point out that it was a very lively discussion, sometimes in English and sometimes in German, with many interruptions and questions, so that the list must not be regarded as more than a general indication and not as anything final. I will give you each of the six points followed by a commentary.

1) When the unconscious is obviously overflowing with fantasies, which is particularly often the case with people who are very rational or intellectual.

In such a case active imagination is not only legitimate but often of the greatest help in establishing a contact with the stored-up unconscious.

However, in such cases there is a certain danger that the unconscious will flow in too rapidly. Often it is indeed no easy task to get such people to accept their fantasies at all, for the more rational and intellectual they are, the more irrational and surprising their fantasies will be. But once they give up their rational prejudice, the fantasies sometimes pour in like a stream which has burst its dam and the people become so fascinated that it makes one feel like an old hen watching her ducklings take to water.

There is also a certain danger with such people—even if they are quite able to stem the flood—of their *indulging* in fantasy. Moreover, they are only too prone to think that once they have learned to let the fantasy flow, they are already doing active imagination; they see the aim as merely establishing the flow. Because of our Western prejudice that thought is insubstantial, it is not generally realized how harmful the indulgence in fantasy can be. We all know extreme cases: how fantasies of being something special, for instance, can rob people of their whole lives as the ordinary people they are.

It is easy to recognize extreme cases, but it is not so generally realized that the same mechanism holds good—in a small and sometimes almost invisible measure—when anyone, however so-called normal, indulges in fantasy, particularly in what we may call wishful fantasy.

I knew a German girl who had constant fantasies of marriage. She was rich, good looking, attractive, but brought up by her mother to think marriage was the only life for a woman. She did not marry because she made every marriageable man she met into the hero of her fantasies, and utterly inhuman these fantasies were because she was possessed on the point, so they naturally always went wrong. She had no sex complex and was perfectly natural with every man who was not marriageable. When in her thirties she at last took matters in hand and went into analysis and soon saw it as a possession. She was able in time to come to terms with that and to sacrifice the demand and even faced unmarried life as a possible fate. Soon after—when she was over forty—she married a very nice man she had known for twenty years. He was at last able to approach her because she was no longer possessed by the desire to marry.

This illustrates the great danger of indulging in fantasy; we may become possessed by our fantasies, which has a bad effect on ourselves and those around us. The possessed possess, or one could also express it: the bewitched bewitch, as one saw so clearly in the case of Hitler, whose rise to power began with his fantasies. As Dr. Jung noted:

> One man, who is obviously "possessed," has infected a whole nation to such an extent that everything is set in motion and has started rolling on its course towards perdition.[25]

Such are the results of indulging in passive or wishful fantasy, but it is of course totally different when we enter the game actively ourselves. Dr. Jung told us a case that night where a girl had brought him a fantasy of a lion in a desert which then turned into a ship on the sea, a car on the road, and so on. She presented this as active imagination but of course he soon told her this was just watching a cinema. She should have questioned the first image, in this case that of the lion in the desert—what did that convey to her and what did she convey to it? Where was *she* in the whole matter? How people set about active imagination is often a useful test as to whether they realize the unconscious as a reality with which they must deal, or whether they think it is so unreal that they can afford to do nothing about it, or whether they believe it is something which one can just put in one's pocket.

If one can really succeed in teaching people to be active in fantasy and to take responsibility for the situations that arise, one need have little or no fear of it doing them any harm. But this is easier said than done and some people have a real block here. This is often a block to be overcome, but not always. Very strong resistances should always be respected, but there is always some resistance. In fact one could here remember what Dr. Jung says in "The Psychology of the Transference": " 'Good advice' is often a doubtful remedy but generally not dangerous because it has so little effect."[26] The same applies as a rule to advice concerning active imagination, because some people love to make fantasy a substitute for the difficulties of life, and then it becomes indulgent and harmful.

I remember when I complained to Dr. Jung about having to give that lecture to the lecturers when I needed all my time to prepare the seminar. He replied briskly: "Well, you could use at least half the time (or for that matter fill a volume) enumerating all the lousy excuses that people make to avoid doing active imagination." I must plead guilty in this respect myself, for I own that I still have to watch very carefully my own "lousy

---

[25] "Wotan," *Civilization in Transition,* CW 10, par. 388.
[26] *The Practice of Psychotherapy,* CW 16, par. 359n.

excuses" for not doing it myself even when I know I should.

One of the "lousy excuses" is having no time, yet—once you get the way of it—it is not very time consuming. A very frequent excuse is that people tell you they are sure they are just making it up and deceiving themselves. It is, of course, always possible to deceive oneself, but usually the idea that they are making it up is quite unfounded. Often they get a shock in this respect. For instance, a man who was experimenting rather half-heartedly with active imagination, suddenly out of a blue sky saw an axe. He wondered where anything so senseless could come from but gave it no further thought. A fortnight later, however, he lost his job, for which the colloquial English expression is "being axed." Now he had known that his business was cutting down staff but he admitted he had not believed it possible that—short of the whole business being closed—his own services could be dispensed with! This made a tremendous impression at the time, but when he got a better job he forgot it so completely that when I asked after his axe some time later, he had the greatest difficulty in recalling the incident at all!

But usually the great deceiver with active imagination is the anima or animus. When once really understood, active imagination puts an end to their power as autonomous demons and, though they themselves are also relieved when this is stopped, it belongs to their nature to do all they can to retain their original power. Dr. Jung once even went so far as to say that active imagination is the touchstone by which one can tell whether someone is genuinely aiming at psychological independence or not! If they *want* to remain a satellite, dependent on their analyst or someone else, that is, secretly and unconsciously dependent on their animus or anima, they will never really devote themselves to the task of active imagination.

2) To reduce the number of dreams when there are too many.

Here you will perhaps excuse my giving an example from my own experience. Once when I had my holidays very late one summer, I went to the mountains by myself, feeling I had earned a complete rest! But I immediately started to dream volumes, in a way I had not dreamed since my earliest analysis. It would have taken all day to write them down! So I did the only thing I knew to stop them: gave up my "complete rest" and started active imagination. This had the desired effect immediately and I had practically no more dreams for the rest of my holiday.

As I was acquainted with the method and had been using it for years, it was of course comparatively easy for me to apply it in this case. But it is more difficult when the person who is drowning in dreams has no idea what to do. A flood of dreams is no certain sign that fantasies will be easily accessible. One is then confronted with the task of teaching that person how to start it and here, in my opinion, it is above all necessary for analysts to know how to do it themselves and to have considerable experience of their own, for ultimately no one will ever take anyone further than one has gone oneself.

In the case of too many dreams, I have found it sometimes works best to take one dream—being very careful that it is one in which the analysand is vitally interested—and begin to ask questions about it. A dream which ends with a question mark is especially useful for this purpose. The more naive and simple such questions are, the more likely they are to produce the desired result. One can also ask oneself such questions if there is no analyst to do it. One should realize that the dream situation is still present somewhere—provided it is a recent dream since older dreams, as you know, usually sink down into the unconscious and are often very difficult to reach again—and then we have to treat the situation as realistically as one would a similar outer situation. At this point it is always necessary for the analyst, if it is being done in analysis, or a person alone, if being done independently, to find the means of expression that suits them best, and then to use it as a point of departure, such as a situation in a dream.

I only mention a situation in a dream as a possible starting point for active imagination because we are speaking of a situation where it is advisable to reduce too many dreams. If there are hypnagogic visions, these usually provide more satisfactory starting points, for visions which occur in the waking state are generally nearer to consciousness than dreams, which may come from a very inaccessible level of the unconscious.

3) A third reason for doing active imagination is when there are too few dreams.

If the dreamlessness has lasted some time, there will probably be no ready-made starting point, and then an even more difficult situation arises in which it may be necessary to *create* a starting point. In Dr. Jung's paper on "The Transcendent Function," written in 1916 while he was still in the early stages of experimenting with active imagination, he said that when there was no starting point, or when no method of approach would work, we could only content ourselves with *what is there.* Usually there is some emotional disturbance, such as anger, depression or even despair. We can then, instead of fighting a bad mood, for instance, concentrate upon it, sink down into it without criticism, lend it the means of expression and do one's best to let it express itself as fully as possible.[27]

I can tell you that this procedure—which was taught to me by Emma Jung as early as 1930—has always been of the very greatest value to me personally. Perhaps it is my Scottish blood, but I love to be able to turn something so apparently useless and even as destructive as a bad mood, a fit of temper or a violent resistance, into something of real value by means of active imagination. I remember once when I thought, with some truth, that I had been treated very unjustly and was near to becoming identical with my negative emotion, I just managed to objectify it enough to be able to hear it say: "If only you can stand me, the eternal water *must* flow." I can only say that that injustice gave me more in the end than any kindness I have ever received.

When there is not even an emotional disturbance the matter is even more difficult, but again one must accept what is there. Perhaps there is a dull feeling of discomfort, resistance, malaise, nausea, boredom or even something quite undefinable. Then, as Dr. Jung suggests in that early paper, a special introversion of the libido is called for, supported by bodily rest. Any quite senseless fragment of fantasy that occurs must be preserved and slowly—very slowly often—a tiny starting point can be fished up from the depths.

4) If someone feels, or seems to be, under indefinable influences, under a sort of spell, or feels or seems to be behind a sort of glass screen.

This losing touch with reality is, as I am sure you all know, one of the most disagreeable phenomena with which one is confronted, both in oneself and in other people, because it is so intangible and baffling. It is a great temptation to use slogans here: "Oh, I am (or he or she is) caught by the animus or anima," or, "It must be an inflation" or a sense of inferiority, or what not. I wasted a lot of time, when I first became really aware of the animus as an undeniable reality, in blaming him for absolutely everything, and being always sure it was his doing when I felt cut off from reality or separated from it by a kind of glass screen.

I remember many years ago getting an awful shock in this respect when

---

[27] [See *Mysterium Coniunctionis*, CW 14, par. 706.—Ed.]

I had worked for weeks diligently on my animus and then, when I saw Dr. Jung again after the holidays, found I had only made matters worse instead of better. For once, the animus was quite blameless and had naturally become very hurt and eventually antagonistic (as everyone in the outer world would also) by my negative assumptions about him. There is nothing more destructive than making negative assumptions. Dr. Jung even once told me that he thought it was the essence of love to give people credit. If one is naive enough to give it where it is not due, he said, it will turn out to be the rope with which they hang themselves, but as a rule it helps people more than anything else one can do for them. The real trouble on this occasion was that something had hurt me in the outer world and instead of admitting it and enduring the suffering involved, I had tried to get above it, understand the person who had hurt me, and so on. My unlived and unrealized emotion had then formed a sort of glass screen between me and the outer world, and I had blamed the animus for cutting me off. Of course this cutting off is certainly a characteristic of the animus, and he is often at the bottom of such a condition, but I mention this incident to show how unwise any such arbitrary conclusion is.

This indefinable screen is a place where active imagination can be pure gold. One should never assume that one knows where such an "indefinable influence," "sort of spell" or "glass screen" comes from—either in itself or other people—but take the condition itself—like the negative emotions, bad moods, and so on which we spoke of before—and try to get it to say what it is. It is true that this is no easy task; such things are often very inarticulate and here again the work will require infinite patience and endurance. But, in my experience at least, if one can give this annoying screen enough credit and avoid negative assumptions about it, in time it will deliver its content, though often in a most incomprehensible image.

At all events, the point I want to make here is that active imagination (where it can be used) is a royal road in dealing with these vague and undefinable influences, for it is the one way—when used well—which leads us inevitably, in the end, to the truth. Of course sometimes we are fortunate enough to have a dream which will clear up the matter, but personally I do not believe in relying blindly on this hope. Our dreams also depend, to some extent, on our attitude toward the unconscious and, if we have drifted into a wrong attitude, we may wait forever for a redemptive dream; only too often the wrong attitude seems to keep them away.

5) When the adaptation to life has been injured.

This, as you know, is a very common cause of people coming into analysis and—in its slighter forms—does not necessarily call for active imagination. Often the dreams and the usual analytical procedure are sufficient to remedy the evil. But when the injury is severe it does not yield to other treatment, and this is one of the conditions where active imagination can be of the most help.

For instance, take the case of an introvert whose adaptation to life has been injured by the demands of an extraverted reality with which he is unable to cope. My own experience suggests that he will only get more and more discouraged—by repeated failures—if he tries to overcome the difficulty directly in the outer world. But if he can overcome the difficulty in the inner world of fantasy—where he is not subject, as a rule, to the feelings of panic which overcome him in the outer world—he will slowly become more self-confident.

In contrast to dreams—where we often find ourselves doing all kinds of things of which we are utterly incapable in the waking state—we usually keep our disabilities in a genuine active imagination. That is, if we try to meet a situation in fantasy which defeats us in the outer world, we often feel as helpless in the one as in the other. The kind of fantasies in which we behave like a hero and utterly unlike our ordinary selves are open to suspicion. They are very often a *phantasia non homo,* as Petronius calls it—a fantasizing out into the blue with no genuine content and no aim except a wish to escape from what we really are into a quite imaginary image of ourselves.

Genuine active imagination, on the other hand, aims at a complete acceptance of what we are—with all our disabilities and faults—but also at an enlargement of the personality by finding out the many other things we also are, which we do not know. Moreover it can reveal the archetypal foundation of which we are a part but with which we must never identify. If, for instance, we indulge in a fantasy of being a hero just because we are particularly cowardly in real life, we have simply identified with the archetype of the hero, and then our fantasy has become *nonhuman,* exactly as Petronius expresses it. But if we play our part in the fantasies—keeping our all-too-human measure—we have a real chance of working things out with the unconscious in a way which will also help us in our daily lives. Here perhaps we need examples to show how an outer situation can be helped practically by an inner procedure like active imagination.

A young man suffered from a phobia concerning the police (a symbol of social adaptation) which lamed his whole life and also prevented him from sleeping, because directly he was in the dark, he became too terrified to sleep. He always tried to overcome this phobia by never giving in to his fear and one night—when he was in a foreign country with insufficient funds—he even borrowed a tent and tried to sleep in a field. He was, however, overcome by panic in the middle of the night and finished the night in a hotel. When he got home, he dreamed that a boxer (the sort of typical strong man at the fair) was walking away from this field in deep dejection.

The young man—who had only a fair to average physique and was moreover a sensitive and slightly effeminate artist—evidently had a strong-man shadow who would not dream of being afraid of the dark and who would be quite capable of dealing with the police. By trying to ignore his fear, he was clearly trying to identify with this shadow—but naturally it did not work for he could not just turn into his own opposite. If he could continue this dream in active imagination, make friends with the man—a rough but by no means ill-natured figure—he would open a door to the possibility of enlarging his personality and of eventually integrating this shadow. But, even before then, through active imagination he could turn this figure into a protector instead of an imaginary assailant. For instance, in the dark—if he was on friendly terms with this shadow—he could ask: "Are you there? Will you help me if anything comes?" Slowly, through such an apparently childish procedure, he could begin to overcome his fear inwardly, which would slowly free him from his crippling sense of inferiority and indirectly help him in his injured adaptation to the outer world.

This man was an introvert. As an example of an extraverted feeling type, I recall the case of a woman who had always adapted easily, or comparatively so, to outer situations. When she was in her forties this adaptation suddenly failed her; everything became difficult and she was soon in an exceedingly neurotic condition. She went into analysis but at first without much effect; if anything she became rather worse. It was only when she began active imagination—which for her took the form of a long and exceedingly interesting series of pictures of very archetypal characters in which she gradually learned to play a role herself—that things began to improve. She had always adapted on a rather superficial level and in time the whole of her energy had secretly flowed into the unconscious, so her outer life became so sterile that she could no longer deal with it.

She was really hopelessly bored with her nearest and dearest though she would rather have died than admit it. When she found a new meaning to life in the fascinating inner images, her earlier extraverted power of dealing with outer situations returned to her, but on a less superficial level. She did not attempt to deal with outer situations inwardly—as the introvert often does perforce—but she followed her missing energy until she found satisfying images which once again gave a meaning to her life and indirectly enabled her to use her natural faculty for extraversion again in the outer world. This healed her injured adaptation.

6) When someone falls into the same hole again and again.

Here Dr. Jung gave us an example that night from his own practice. A woman complained that she had just fallen into the same hole again as she had been doing all her life, so he told her that at last she must ask herself: why? She must ask the unconscious and then patiently wait for whatever came. At last, after about three weeks, she reported that she saw a wall. She was standing before this wall and was unable to get anything to move. He asked her: "Well, what are you going to do about it?" At last she came on the idea that there might be a door. Then she looked up and down the wall but there was none. Dr. Jung asked her every time he saw her: "Well, what about that wall, when on earth are you going to do something about it?" He added: "I swore at her even, the stupid cow." This lasted for three weeks and then she discovered one might take a hammer and chisel and make a hole in the wall. It took her another three weeks to break through and come out on the other side when at last she was able to see what it was all about.

This gives us some idea of the patience required in a case of this kind. Once one is really sure active imagination is indicated, one must never give way. It is usually avoided because of the responsibility involved, for in active imagination, done as it should be done, you cannot avoid responsibility. You must make your own decisions and you soon find out that it is no harmless game, for what one does in active imagination affects one's whole character and life. If this woman had not found the way to break through this wall in herself, there would have been no chance of her breaking the spell—whatever it was—that attracted her into the same hole again and again.

*

It is an impossible task to give a complete description of active imagination in one lecture, therefore this must necessarily be full of omissions and terribly fragmentary. However, I have tried to give you some idea of what active imagination entails and the far-reaching effects it may have. This is undoubtedly a very difficult idea for our Western prejudices, which are inclined to dismiss thought and fantasy as something that, however interesting or even fascinating they may be in themselves, have no material existence or direct effect on outer life. Dr. Jung once pointed out, when trying to make this point clear, that there is nothing in this room or house that was not first a thought in someone's mind. When we truly realize that, we begin to understand the depth of our responsibility for our own thoughts and fantasies. Dr. Jung's own sense of responsibility was so strong that during his odyssey into the unconscious he gave up his post of lecturer at the university, for, as he says,

> The material brought to light from the unconscious had, almost literally, struck me dumb. . . . It would be unfair to continue teaching young students when my own intellectual situation was nothing but a mass of doubts.[28]

It was finding "the place and purpose" in actual life of the things Dr. Jung discovered in active imagination that led him inexorably into such a highly active life, so different from the one of learned leisure that he longed for. He found himself swamped with patients from all over the world, with increased obligations and commitments to lecture and give seminars. He says himself that he had "hit upon this stream of lava" in the unconscious, and "the heat of its fires reshaped my life."[29] The work on these images from the unconscious was for him "an extremely long-drawn-out affair, and it was only after some twenty years of it that I reached some degree of understanding my fantasies."[30] And more:

> It has taken me virtually forty-five years to distill within the vessel of my scientific work the things I experienced and wrote down at that time.
>   . . . The later details are only supplements and clarifications of the material that burst forth from the unconscious. . . . It was the *prima materia* for a lifetime's work.[31]

---

[28] *Memories, Dreams, Reflections,* p. 193.
[29] Ibid., p. 199.
[30] Ibid., p. 200.
[31] Ibid., p. 199.

Whether we know it or not, our own fantasies and active imagination are also the *prima materia* of our lives and will shape them for good or ill. For good if—in our own small way—we distill them in the vessel of our work and do our utmost to find their "place and purpose" in our own actual lives. But most certainly for ill if we do not take this responsibility on ourselves and instead allow ourselves to be possessed by them. Then, to a greater or lesser degree, sooner or later, we should meet the fate of being possessed by power, of which Hitler is perhaps a classic example but only one among the multitude which unfortunately we see on all sides today.

3
Regression or Renewal in Later Life

This manuscript was given to me by Miss Hannah during the course of my analysis with her. To my knowledge, it has never before appeared in print. Her permission to publish it has given us all a rare treasure. Because Miss Hannah herself came from a family of clergy, she always had a soft spot in her heart for analysands who were theologians, or whose vocations were allied to the institutional Church.

It was not her practice to betray professional confidences, in fact she was very circumspect in this regard. However, she apparently felt that the person referred to in this paper represented a classic case of mid-life transition. She did not tell me why she gave it to me to read—I knew! I also knew that there were many others with a theological background who endured struggles similar to those of "George."

This case material is presented here as a record of one person's pursuit of wholeness, how the analyst was involved in the process, and the dreams which fueled the endeavor.

A great many people come to analysis when the *Weltanschauung* or world-view that has carried them successfully, or at any rate tolerably, through the earlier stages of their life, is wearing thin. The approach of old age, or even of the second half of life, leaves many people confronted with the fact that their interests or pleasures no longer suffice, and they begin to ask themselves whether they are not missing the real meaning of their life.

This crisis can take innumerable forms and the case I want to describe is just one of these. Like all the others, it has a collective side: a man of fifty-eight was confronted with finding a new and broader *Weltanschauung,* and a highly individual side. Life had led him into an impasse which, because of his character and circumstances, was his unique problem. Just as every individual has hands basically similar to every other human being, and yet fingerprints which can be traced only to that individual among all the millions of the human species, so every human fate is, in a way, basically similar and yet entirely different and even absolutely unique.

Before we turn to this case I should perhaps make a few general remarks about the problem of aging in general.

Jung has said in many places that the first half of life is the time when outer life is all-important. But when the middle of life is reached, the direction changes: the goal that was life becomes death and the inner life is then as all-important as the outer was before. Of course there is no neat boundary; outer things or tasks can be vitally important even at a very advanced age and people can be faced with a religious problem, apparently belonging to the inner life, at a very early age. It is more a matter of the general attitude to life: in the first half of life, broadly speaking, we need to find out what outer life is—in and for itself—and, in the second, what inner life is—in and for itself—which latter, of course, includes trying to discover the meaning and purpose of our outer life.

In his BBC "Face to Face" telecast in 1959, Jung was asked by John Freeman what advice he would give to old people to enable them to live properly, when most of them in fact believe that death is the end of everything. He replied:

> Well, you see, I have treated many old people and it's quite interesting to watch what the unconscious is doing with the fact that it is apparently threatened with a complete end. It disregards it. Life behaves as if it were going on, and so I think it is better for an old person to live on, to look forward to the next day, as if he had to spend centuries, and then he lives properly. But when he is afraid, when he doesn't look forward, he looks back, he petrifies, he gets stiff and he dies before his time: but when he's living and looking forward to the great adventure that is ahead, then he lives, and that is about what the unconscious is intending to do.[32]

This really sums up our theme in a nutshell. If we look back, regretting our youth and seeing no reality but the concrete—which eludes us more day by day—we petrify, regress, become irritable, afraid and unhappy, like the aging animal so well described in Ernest Thompson Seton's *Biography of a Grizzly*. The end of that book contains a perfect description of the end of any human life that has chosen the path of regression.

But how can we understand the other alternative mentioned by Jung? How can we look forward to the next day as if we had centuries before us, regarding death as the great adventure to come, as a goal and not an end?

Obviously this is mainly a matter of experience and does not lend itself to words. But I think most people know at some level that they have experienced such things, and could again, were it possible for them to overcome their ingrained rational and concrete point of view. Indeed, many people are not troubled by the rational but they tend to swim above life

---

[32] *C.G. Jung Speaking*, p. 438.

and miss the value of the here and now. Again there is no sharp division between these two attitudes, for they often exist simultaneously in the same individual.

A woman who was trying to realize this unknown, eternal side of the psyche in active imagination, was told by an inner figure that she either forgot all about the center, the Self, or identified with it, when she swam aimlessly in the center. But she should be constantly aware of the center from a firm place (her daily life), because only when she stayed there could the center itself work through her.

In order to make clearer how I understand this "living as if we had centuries to spend," I should like to give a short excerpt from a lecture of Jung's at the E.T.H. (Eidgenössische Technische Hochshule) in Zurich in 1941, where he was speaking of the necessity of self-knowledge. He was analyzing the "Empress" poem in the "Rosarium Philosophorum," where the alchemist-poet says that the *lapis* can only be built by the man who can see through himself. Jung said:

> As to this self knowledge, this real penetrating knowledge of our own being, do not make the mistake of thinking that it means seeing through the ego. To understand the ego is child's play, but to see through the Self is something totally different. The real difficulty lies in recognizing the unknown. No one need remain ignorant of the fact that he is striving for power, that he wants to become very rich, that he would be a tyrant if he had the chance, that he is pleasure seeking, envious of other people, and so on. Everyone *can* know such things of him or herself, because they are mere ego knowledge. But Self knowledge is something completely different, it is learning to know of the things which are unknown.[33]

He goes on to give an idea of these unknown things in the language of the poem: a knowledge of the spiritual, even divine, side of man that alone can lead to that union of the opposites that is the *conditio sine qua non* of the *lapis philosophorum*. In these lectures Jung defines the *lapis*—the product for which the alchemists strove so unceasingly—as "an optimum of the life process or as the idea of an optimum."[34] It seems to me that he has described this optimum anew in his telecast as living each day as if we had centuries to spend.

---

[33] "Alchemy: The Process of Individuation—Notes on Lectures Given at the Eidgenössische Technische Hochschule, Zürich, 1940-41," p. 72.
[34] Ibid., p. 68.

Naturally this does not mean losing ourselves in metaphysical speculations about eternity. It means the terrific effort of realizing that we are not just conscious egos but part and parcel of the eternal Self. Obviously such a realization is not the problem of everyone who comes into analysis, particularly not of most young people. Here we must take into consideration the fact that our case is a minister who was thus forced from the beginning, by his very profession, to consider the eternal aspect of life. In our materialistic days, this aspect is probably less in evidence than in any previous age, which certainly adds to our difficulty in "recognizing the unknown," because it is now more unknown than ever before.

Our case, therefore, gives us a good opportunity to see the almost superhuman effort that is required to realize this unknown side of ourselves. This man of fifty-eight was in the throes of this problem when death overtook him. From the physical side it was entirely unexpected. He died suddenly of a heart attack without knowing, or at any rate without telling me, that he had any reason to spare his heart. But psychologically there had been indications. In fact, looking back, it almost seems as if the unconscious was offering him the choice between regression or renewal, but it is easy to be wise *after* the event and much more difficult before. That a basic change was inevitable was quite obvious, but whether that change was in life or death, I had no idea. Under the circumstances it is of course impossible to ask his permission to use his material—my invariable rule in such cases—but, as he had a quite unusual love of humanity, I feel almost sure that he would be willing and even glad if anyone could learn something useful from his experience.

George Brown—we will call him—was a Scotsman, born and brought up near Edinburgh. His family was well off but, apart from pleasant outer surroundings, he had a rough deal from the beginning. He was the youngest of a large family of boys and, when he was only three, his parents separated. The elder boys went with the father but George was left—rather as one might leave a Pekinese dog—to be a comfort to the mother! Whenever she got tired of him, however, she sent him to his father where he was seriously bullied by his older brothers, especially by one of them. He told me he thus never knew where he belonged.

Almost miraculously, George nevertheless grew up to be an exceedingly manly little boy, excelling at all kinds of sports. The rougher kind had to be kept a secret from his mother and she only learned from the newspapers, when he achieved international fame, that he had deceived her in this respect. Her annoyance at having been disobeyed greatly outweighed any pleasure or pride in his achievements, which gives us a useful insight into their relationship.

The parents reacted in opposite ways to their disappointment in marriage. The father decided to have nothing more to do with women and lived his life ignoring them as much as possible: whereas the mother filled her life with numerous men friends. George—who was naturally much tied to his beautiful mother—suffered agonies of jealousy and was terrified that she would marry again. She did, but not until he was eighteen.

The father was as kind as his embittered life allowed but the only people from whom George received real human warmth and kindness were the servants. It is, therefore, not surprising that his first love was a young maid servant of his mother's. The girl was the daughter of a respectable farmer and George's father overcame his prejudice against women to the extent of saying he would not oppose it if George decided to marry the girl. (In the father's morality any relation other than marriage between the sexes was simply nonexistent.) The mother, however, was socially ambitious and opposed it bitterly. George's life in her house had anyhow become impossible for she extracted the same obedience from him as when he was a child, and with all this conflict about the girl, he decided to emigrate to the United States and send for the girl when he had earned enough money of his own. He was then twenty-three years old.

George had been brought up to his father's trade. The latter was the owner of an old-established firm of hand-made boots and shoes of world-wide fame. George—who had been through the works—was particularly gifted at this trade. He was, however, the youngest son, so his father made no particular objection to his trying his fortune in New York. He had only to enter the best establishments on Fifth Avenue—with a pair of shoes made by himself in his hand—to obtain first-rate employment. Everything seemed set for a steady rise in his trade with a fortune as the goal.

But then fate took a hand in the game. George met a doctor who impressed him very much and this man opened his eyes to the fact that in America you *chose* your own profession and did not necessarily remain in the father's line of business. Such a revolutionary idea had never even entered his head, and for the first time it occurred to him that perhaps there might be professions which would interest him more than his own. In his enthusiasm for his new friend, he decided to use his savings to study to become a doctor. But when he was a student, he had a religious experience which decided him to become a minister.

I have forgotten the name of the church which he joined—it is not a well-known one—and perhaps this is just as well, for I did not get a very good impression of it. In the middle of his studies for the ministry, he had a letter from his girlfriend in Europe speaking of other men, which upset him so much that he used the long vacation to work his way back to Europe in order to see her. But he found her adamant: he was on a path where he saw no financial security and she was not one to risk all for love, if indeed she loved him at all. This was a shattering blow to him at the time.

A few years later, while still studying in America, he met an exceedingly pretty girl, with whom he was thrown together a good deal. Other men warned him there was something wrong but—as he supposed later—he did not want to hear. At all events, one day he was moved to give her a very chaste kiss and that settled it: he *knew* beyond all doubt that when you kissed a girl you married her! His doubts as to any chance of happiness in the marriage indeed increased daily, especially when the girl retired to a nursing home with an obvious mental breakdown but—as he was now ordained— his ecclesiastical authorities told him he must leave the ministry if he broke his plighted word to the girl and after all there was that kiss! So he stifled his healthy instinct, refused to listen to his friends outside the church, and married her.

Of course his marriage was a failure from the beginning. They had one perfectly healthy child but his wife's mental instability became more and more marked. To cut a long story short, at last he had to confine her to a mental hospital.

In the meantime he was doing exceedingly well in his profession. He got on very well with men and—though he had some disappointments in friendship owing to his extreme naiveté—he was exceedingly popular. Women also were always running after him—as they so often do after parsons—but they never succeeded in breaking through his strictly professional persona.

This went on until George was in his middle fifties but then his childish faith in God—as an all-loving Father who would bring everything right in the end—began to show signs of wearing thin. He had caught himself thinking: "Can God be so good and just, if He treats such a well-meaning chap as myself in such a way?" Or "Do I really at bottom believe all the comforting things I preach?" At first he repressed such thoughts sternly, assured himself that everything which had happened to him was undoubtedly his own fault and did his best to attribute all good to God and all evil to himself. It was in the middle of this conflict that he came across Dr. Jung's "Answer to Job." He tried hard to have the typical theological reaction, but he found himself reading it again and again, until he almost knew it by heart.

At the same time he got into difficulties in his work. By this time he had risen to a good position in the church and was also chaplain at a large hospital where he gave some kind of psychological treatment, under a doctor's supervision, to a number of the hospital patients and also to some of his parishioners. At first this seems to have gone smoothly but the difficulties began when he discovered he was not immune to the dangers of countertransference! To cut a long story short, he found himself very much attracted by one of his most difficult cases, a very beautiful girl, some thirty years younger than himself.

As the anima, she represented the energy of life itself, and was thus of vital importance to him. But he was inclined to misunderstand the meaning and to identify her with all he had missed in life. Thus the thought of her became a temptation to regard himself still as a young man with his life before him, able to meet and solve all his problems in outer life. One could say that this was George's main difficulty: although he kept repeating that he was fifty-eight, he did not truly realize that he was in the second and not the first half of life. This is—in my experience at least—a very common attitude, but it is unfortunate, to say the least.

George did not analyze without having been analyzed himself but he had a very naive attitude to what he called "therapy." You just found a therapist, put a penny in the slot, and drew out the cure! But when it came to his tormenting religious problem and to the problem of his "countertransference," he felt no wish to go back to any of his previous analysts. (I never found out anything about them, except that they were neither Freudians nor Jungians.) He decided to ask for a year's leave of absence and come to Zurich. This decision, he told me, was taken entirely on account of the impression that "Answer to Job" had made on him.

The unconscious was just a word in Jung's books to George when he came to Zurich. He also had no practical experience of dreams. Two earlier dreams, however, had made a great impression on him because he had dreamed both frequently over a period of years:

1. He was flying round and round in the air as if he were swimming. (This dream was rather pleasant but the second was very disagreeable.)

2. He found himself in a busy city with many people around and discovered that he was only wearing a shirt, with no pants, and was always terrified that the people would look at him.

The first dream was evidently telling him his exact state: he was swimming above reality and—from the fact that he found it pleasant—was evidently quite unconscious that anything was wrong in this respect. About many things in the world of men he was exceedingly practical and apparently very much on the earth, so it was difficult for him to realize. Moreover, he was very much on the lookout for any inflation and was very careful *not* to think that he was better than any other men because he was a clergyman. But it soon became apparent that, in a very subtle way, he was deceiving himself in this respect. If I said,: "Oh well, this or that is only human," he would reply, "Oh I know, but you see I have always known *I* must not do, say or think about it." So secretly he was setting himself a superhuman standard and thus flying above the human level.

This also throws light on the second dream. Such illusions would be rudely dispelled were he to come down to the human-all-too-human level. The beautiful persona—and it was a real work of art that he had built up so diligently—would unaccountably be missing and particularly his lower parts would be exposed. He would be revealed as an ordinary human being, made just like any other man.

The first dreams in his analysis with me were all concerned with his personal shadow and with dispelling his illusion that he could ask more of himself than of other people. He had unusual courage and a great willingness to suffer, and he showed me how true it is that "it is mere child's play to understand" the shadow and the whole sphere of the ego. He made the most rapid progress I have ever witnessed in this realm.

One thing, however, worried both him and myself from the beginning. He was very much struck by Jung's emphasis on the end of Christ's saying: "Thou shalt love thy neighbor *as thyself,*" and saw intellectually that it was impossible for him really to love his neighbor until he loved himself. Yet his whole life had been built up by loving his neighbor. He used to say almost every analytical hour: "I can't love myself, I can't." His mother—in his earliest youth—had cut the ground from under his feet in this respect: she had *not* believed in him and his own long habit of not believing in himself was inaccessible to reason.

I sometimes wished that the unconscious would not be quite so ruthless in rubbing in his shadow right through his early dreams, as I was afraid it would make him dislike himself more. But this was not the case. It was not his bad qualities that upset him; once he saw that he was as other men, he was quite willing to extend the same tolerance to himself that he had always had for other people. It is, however, a very common prejudice to think that the personal shadow contains only undesirable qualities, whereas sometimes our very best qualities are discovered when we explore the personal unconscious. Jung even said once in a seminar that it is possible to find up to eighty percent pure gold in the shadow. Although George was most willing to see the dark side of his nature when it was rubbed in by his dreams, I noticed that he was always rather embarrassed when better qualities were hinted at. Such qualities have usually been repressed because one does not want to take responsibility for them, for good qualities and talents always carry a certain obligation. I think the real trouble here was that he had repressed a lot of pure gold and that he did not want to be as much as he might have been, so he preferred not to love himself, even to reject himself.

After George had done a great deal of conscientious work on his shadow, he had the following dream:

> He was helping a farmer move from a low-lying farm to one that stood on higher ground. There were two cars and he drove one up to the higher farm and put it in the garage. He thought the farmer might really deal with the second but, as he did not like to suggest it, he returned to the lower farm to fetch it. There he saw the waters had been rising rapidly and that a great deal of manure—which had been put on the lawn—was rapidly turning into a muddy swamp. But the new farmer in the lower farm was delighted, and said that the land would really be fertile now.

His associations: Both the farmers were sturdy honest men such as he had known and loved in his boyhood. His happiest holidays had been spent on farms, riding and doing land work. But his wife's people had had a farm in America, and he had been so unhappy there that it had spoiled his early recollections. In the dream he recaptured his old love for farms and he spent quite a lot of time afterward painting the two farms and imagining himself there. He associated the manure—put down by the outgoing farmer—to the fact that he always felt compelled to spend a lot of money on a house he was leaving, so that the new occupants would be fully satisfied.

This dream marked the end of the first stage in George's analysis. For the moment, he had done all he could in his personal psychology. He had, to quote the words in Jung's E.T.H. lecture, seen that behind his very real consideration for other people he was striving for power over them, that he wanted to become very rich, that he was envious of other people who had been able to live a fuller life than he and that the desire for pleasure—to make up for all he had missed in his youth—was playing a far greater role in his countertransference than he had realized. The dream conveyed to him the value of mud—of all those disagreeable realizations—and that there was someone in him who could make this the basis for a new growth.

George also realized that he had another side which had gained a higher standpoint in the new farm above the floods, symbolizing that higher point of view from which we can sometimes look down on our problems as if they were a thunderstorm in the valley below us. Moreover, he was, or was capable of being, on good terms with both the farmers, "sturdy, honest men," and he had two cars at his disposal with which he could circulate freely between them. This dream synchronized with some outer positive events and, for the first time, he felt much happier about himself. "Perhaps I am not such a bad chap after all," he said, which was no mean achievement, considering the all too human qualities he had just seen in himself for the first time and his lifelong tendency to depreciate himself.

But his deeper problems were by no means solved. Although he had found a new attitude to his own dark side, the same did not apply to God, who was still not allowed to have any shadow at all! He was beginning, though reluctantly, to see that he couldn't decide what to do about whether he should remain in the ministry and his other problems from the conscious alone, that we should have to ascertain what the deeper unconscious had to say about it. This, as I pointed out to him, was equivalent to finding out what God's will was in these matters, and if he was so convinced that God was an all-loving Father, why was he so afraid of what God might want? He was a very honest man and admitted he was not that sure!

The next striking dream took him right down into the depths:

> A very large ship had sunk some time ago in very deep water and the dreamer had the task of going down as a diver to explore the ship and to

bring up any valuables he might find. He should also investigate whether the ship might be refloated. He had the right equipment, could carry out his task but—when it was finished—he noticed that the oxygen was getting low. The oxygen was in a sort of main tube: not just his oxygen, but that of other people as well. There was sufficient for him to reach the surface, but ought he to take it all? Other people might still be in the ship and require it—he thought specifically of his child and this girl? He woke up at this point quite uncertain what to do.

The large ship he associated to his previous way of navigating on the sea: the unconscious. He had lived close to the sea as a boy, and had been a great deal in ships. He was willing to consider the possibility, therefore, that this ship might be the ship of the Church which had carried him safely and happily in his youth but had sunk some time before.[35] Even before he came to Zurich, he really knew that this had happened but he was still quite uncertain whether to go on as if it were still floating, for the sake of other people, to die with them, so to speak, rather than take their oxygen, or to give it up entirely. The new idea in this dream, and one which was very disagreeable to him, was that he could not just leave it at the bottom of the sea, for it contained values that could not be spared and he was commanded to investigate them, at enormous personal risk. Possibly it should even be refloated.

Here George was very much hindered by a *deformation professionnelle.* Nearly every theologian, confronted by doubts as to the doctrine he has preached and believed, wants to do one of two things: cut his losses and leave the Church entirely, or repress his doubts and continue in the minis-

---

[35] Hugo Rahner in his "Antenna Crucis, III, The Wooden Ship" has collected a great number of passages mainly from the Patristic literature where the Church is represented as a ship because "it is steered by God and is the continuation of the victory over all ungodly powers won by Christ on the wooden cross." For example, St. Ambrose in his "De virginitate" 18, 118 (PL 16 297B) summed up the essence and fate of the Church in the words: "In hoc bene navigat mundo." Rahner says St. Ambrose spoke with the whole pride of a Roman Christian who compares his Church with the good ships in the time of the Imperial peace when they sailed from Alexandria, Constantinople and Carthage to the port of Rome. "No, the ship of the Church," says St. Ambrose, "is anything but despicable as it rides the high seas with its sails spread from the mast of the cross and filled by the stormy wind of the Holy Ghost." Innumerable other examples are to be found in Rahner's article, which is printed in *Zeithschrift für Katholische Theologie,* vol. 66 (1942), pp. 196ff.

try. The priests or clergymen willing to think out this problem in all its ramifications are very rare. This dream could be called a typical theologian's dream, presenting, in whatever outer form, the choice of coming to terms with the problem, a very difficult but highly rewarding task which leads to a real renewal, or denying its existence, which leads to regression and, when they then seem bound to regress, a death which is either spiritual or physical.

We find the same idea in the next dream:

> George was moving to a distant town and was bustling about trying to deal with his books. He longed to abandon them, either to leave them with his friend who had them or to put them in storage. At the height of his despair, the solid heavy bookcases suddenly became collapsible and light enough for him to carry himself.

His books, about six hundred, were mainly theological and had lost their value for him. He had actually loaned them to the friend in the dream. Evidently this dream carries on the idea of the values left in the ship of the Church. However much he wants to abandon them, he cannot. But if he tackles the problem honestly, a miracle happens, the heavy and cumbersome becomes light and the problem is suddenly solved. Instead of just throwing over his previous beliefs, he must evidently think them out, and provide them with a new foundation, the shelves. Then he will be able to take the essence of all those cumbersome things with him—even carried under his arm—to the new, far away town, which would symbolize a completely new attitude and standpoint.

We see now why "Answer to Job" was such a bombshell in his life. Unbeknown at the time to him, the ship of his Church had sunk as far as he was concerned. There is no question of sabotage, it was an event—a "just-so story"— beyond his control. But that is not the end of the story. The farmer (in George), who lived in the upper farm, was a genuinely religious man and the question of God and his attitude to God remained, however much his faith in the Church had foundered. But there was also the farmer in the lower farm who was still passionately interested in the things of this life and in making up for the things George had missed. When a great deal of life has not been lived, this is usually a red hot problem, particularly at his age.

George did not take very kindly to the task of thinking out the whole problem of his religious life. Thinking was his inferior function and it is well known how difficult things become when that is involved. But he was an intelligent man and the idea in the dreams was fairly clear to him. The resistance I think came mainly from his fear of what God might require of him.

At this point there was an interesting synchronistic event. He had just acquired a small second-hand car and came out in it to his hours with me. We live close to the big road along the lake and there is an official parking place on the other side of the road. George wanted to park his car there and was very careful, not only to put out his blinker but to check to see if anything was coming from behind. Satisfied that there was not, he turned right and collided with a car coming in the other direction! No one was hurt but both cars were rather badly damaged. He arrived exceedingly upset, for he had driven without an accident for many years and this was undeniably his own fault. He had just turned into a stream of traffic without looking. Synchronistic events were very important to George, so he was most anxious to see just what this one meant in his psychology.

We decided that it did correspond to his problem very closely. His great difficulty was to realize—in everyday life, not in the Church—that he was *not* master in his own house, that there was another will in his psyche that was often moving in exactly the opposite direction to where he wanted to go. This was really at the bottom of his fear of finding out God's will, for He might, and probably would, want something quite different from what George wanted. So he kept ignoring this "other will," this something in him going in the opposite direction, and now he had actually smashed up his car by not looking that way.

This made a great impression on him, but he didn't like it. He hated the fact that he was ignoring the other direction to the extent of having his first car accident, and he hated still more the idea that the other will was so strong, that it could apparently manifest in this way.

At this point he had the dream which impressed him the most of all his dreams. He dreamed:

> He met a woman at a party of his relatives whom he realized at once was *the* woman he had always been looking for but never met in outer life. She was beautiful and very attractive physically but it was more than that. He felt at once she was the essence of relationship, completely self-contained and independent of him and yet fully related. Wherever she went she held out her hand to him and evidently enjoyed his company but felt there was no touch of constraint. He felt completely free and natural

with her. They went to a store downtown together and every moment was a joy.

It was clear from these dreams that George was faced with not only the task of thinking out his religious problem, but also with the most difficult of all problems for a man: the confrontation with the anima. Of course, it was obvious from the start that his anima was projected onto the girl. The dreams gave me an excellent opportunity to draw his attention to Jung's writings on the subject.

Perhaps the clearest and simplest of all Jung's descriptions of the anima is to be found in chapter 3 of *Aion,* "The Syzygy: Anima and Animus." Jung says there:

> What, then, is this projection-making factor? The East calls it the "Spinning Woman"—Maya, who creates illusion by her dancing. Had we not long since known it from the symbolism of dreams, this hint from the Orient would have put us on the right track: the enveloping, embracing, and devouring element points unmistakably to the mother, that is, to the son's relation to the real mother, to her imago, and to the woman who is to become a mother for him. His Eros is passive like a child's; he hopes to be caught, sucked in, enveloped, and devoured. He seeks, as it were, the protecting, nourishing, charmed circle of the mother, the condition of the infant released from every care, in which the outside world bends over him and even forces happiness upon him. No wonder the real world vanishes from sight![36]

Jung goes on to describe the mother complex which ties a son to his mother through the myth of the *hieros gamos.* He then says:

> This myth, better than any other, illustrates the nature of the collective unconscious. At this level the mother is both old and young. Demeter and Persephone, and the son is spouse and sleeping suckling rolled into one. The imperfections of real life, with its laborious adaptations and manifold disappointments, naturally cannot compete with such a state of indescribable fulfillment.
>
> In the case of the son, the projection-making factor is identical with the mother-imago, and this is consequently taken to be the real mother. The projection can only be dissolved when the son sees that in the realm of his psyche there is an image not only of the mother but of the daughter, the sister, the beloved, the heavenly goddess, and the chthonic Baubo. Every mother and every beloved is forced to become the carrier and embodiment of this omnipresent and ageless image, which corre-

---

[36] CW 9ii, par. 20.

sponds to the deepest reality in a man. It belongs to him, this perilous image of Woman; she stands for the loyalty which in the interest of life he must sometimes forego; she is the much needed compensation for the risks, struggles, sacrifices that all end in disappointment; she is the solace for all the bitterness of life. And, at the same time, she is the great illusionist, the seductress, who draws him into life with her Maya—and not only into life's reasonable and useful aspects, but into its frightful paradoxes and ambivalences where good and evil, success and ruin, hope and despair, counterbalance one another. Because she is his greatest danger she demands from a man his greatest, and if he has it in him she will receive it. . . .

I deliberately and consciously give preference to a dramatic, mythological way of thinking and speaking, because this is not only more expressive but also more exact than an abstract scientific terminology, which is wont to toy with the notion that its theoretic formulations may one fine day be resolved into algebraic equations.

The projection-making factor is the anima, or rather the unconscious as represented by the anima. Whenever she appears, in dreams, visions and fantasies, she takes on personified form, thus demonstrating that the factor she embodies possesses all the outstanding characteristics of a feminine being. She is not an invention of the conscious, but a spontaneous product of the unconscious. Nor is she a substitute figure for the mother. On the contrary, there is every likelihood that the numinous qualities which make the mother-imago so dangerously powerful derive from the collective archetype of the anima, which is incarnated anew in every male child.[37]

One could amplify this figure of the anima endlessly. A particularly well-known example is that of Dante's Beatrice. Dante saw the real woman only once but his creative genius was able to regain the projection and to describe man's inner positive anima in an unsurpassed way in his *Divine Comedy*. Petrarch's *Laura* is another such figure and, in more modern times, Rider Haggard's *She*. But the example which came vividly to my mind while George was telling me the dream of his anima taking him downtown, was that of Socrates. On one of the last evenings of his life, while in prison, Socrates dreamed that a bright, beautiful feminine figure appeared and called to him "O Socrates, the third day hence to cloddy [or "clayey," meaning fruitful] Phythia shalt thou come." Socrates drew the conclusion that this meant death, which brings us to the anima in her death-aspect, to the *Todeshochzeit* (death-marriage) as it is called in Ger-

---

[37] Ibid., pars. 23ff.

man, an archetypal motif which one could also amplify endlessly.

The best-known modern example, frequently quoted by Jung, is Benoit's *L'Atlantide* in which the anima—living in a beautiful faraway castle—has a mausoleum of the young men who have died by her means on their bridal night. Leo also dies in Rider Haggard's *Ayesha*, in his first embrace with the anima.

The archetypal motif of the *Todeshochzeit* was even exalted to the central theme of the last chapter of the medieval alchemical text called "Aurora Consurgens," as Marie-Louise von Franz points out in her book on this text.[38] She mentions several old authorities on the theme and points out that death was described as a mystical marriage in the Cabala, and quotes the following passage from the Zohar:

> At the funeral of the Rabbi Schim'on ben Jochaii, the disciples heard a voice saying: "Up, come and gather together for the marriage of Rabbi Schim'on: peace be with you and they may rest on their couches."[39]

Jung points out in *Symbols of Transformation* that St. Augustine actually interprets Christ's death as a *hieros gamos* with the mother, similar to the feast of Adonis, where Venus and Adonis were laid on the bridal couch:

> Like a bridegroom Christ went forth from his chamber, he went out with a presage of his nuptials into the field of the world. . . . He came to the marriage-bed of the cross, and there, in mounting it, he consummated his marriage. And when he perceived the sighs of the creature, he lovingly gave himself up to the torment in place of his bride, and he joined himself to the woman (matrona) for ever.[40]

Honorius of Autun describes the crucifixion as a mortal wound of love which Christ received for the sake of the Church, in order to make her his bride on his death bed.[41] It is well known that Thomas Aquinas studied the "Song of Solomon" on his death bed, which again shows this typical combination of death and the love union with the anima. We also find the motif of the *Todeshochzeit* in many variations in folklore which, according to Jung, "means that the unconscious psyche often depicts death as a union of the opposites, that is, as an inner becoming whole."[42]

---

[38] *Aurora Consurgens,* pp. 362ff.

[39] Ibid., p. 428.

[40] CW 5, par. 411.

[41] Honorius Autun, *Exposit in Cant. Cant. Migne,* P.L. tom. 172, p. 419.

[42] *Aurora Consurgens,* p. 428.

To return to the theme of Socrates' dream which was the first amplification of George's dream that came to my mind. As I already mentioned, Socrates himself drew the justifiable conclusion that his dream meant death. But, as Marie-Louise von Franz pointed out in her paper on this dream, it could also have meant that it was now time for Socrates to face the whole problem of the mother complex and the anima.[43] In some ways Socrates' position was not unlike that of George, for both had put masculine righteousness above the problem of heterosexual eros.

These amplifications of George's dream have made it clearer. The anima, by throwing off her projection on the actual girl and appearing as the woman he had always been looking for but had never found in outer life, has revealed herself as his own soul image, as the inner anima. George's eros was still contained in his mother complex, so his task was very much the one described by Jung in the passage quoted earlier from chapter 3 of *Aion*. He was indeed completely fascinated for some weeks by the woman in his dream. He found a picture in a magazine of a woman who resembled her, carried it around with him and spoke of her constantly. For a time the actual woman by whom he had been attracted faded out completely, and he hoped eagerly to meet in outer life the woman of his dream. He found it very difficult to realize her as an *inner* figure; in fact, looking back, I do not think that this aspect was real to him at all.

One does frequently meet with such a real ingrained difficulty in men. Since the beginning it has been man's task to deal with outer reality. He guarded the camp in prehistoric times, and had to watch for the slightest movement that might indicate the approach of an enemy. Woman, on the other hand, was inside the cave or camp, cooking and looking after the children and so on. She could afford to have inner fantasies, for she was guarded outside, but man could not. Therefore one must always be very careful not to force a man to see the inner anima too quickly; it is against a healthy instinct in him.

As to the death-marriage aspect, for a short time I did realize that the anima might well intend to take George to the Beyond if he did not face the religious problem set by the two preceding dreams and the existence of the anima. I tried to put this aspect before him but, as I have said, he had a tremendous resistance to facing the question of what his previous faith still

---

[43] [See *On Dreams and Death: A Jungian Interpretation*, pp. 52f.—Ed.]

meant to him. He talked about the anima rather glibly which, of course, he could not have done had she really been a reality to him with the power of life and death in her hands. But I see now (it is easy to be wise after the event) that I should have insisted much more than I did on the possibility of physical death, and I should have dwelt more on the theme of the death-marriage, for Socrates' dream was brought up by my own unconscious while George was actually telling me his dream. But he was an extraordinarily healthy man, very masculine and still engaged in every kind of sport, so it was somehow very difficult to associate him with death. I let myself be reassured by the fact that the anima took him downtown and hoped, as he did, that this meant she was going to lead him to a new and more meaningful stage in inner, and perhaps also outer, reality.

In short, at this time, in spite of my momentary realization that his dream might be referring to actual death, I really had no idea that there was any immediate danger.

In addition, George began to understand that it was going to take him longer that he had thought to work out his problem, and started to make plans to return to Zurich for a longer period and, if possible, to take the diploma at the Institute. Although I was uncertain whether this was practicable at his age, I thought that a thorough study of Jungian psychology for an outer purpose might give him just the opportunity he required for his inner need—to move the essence of his theological books to the distant town of his new Jungian attitude, and to learn about the anima. Thus I did not oppose his plan. Outwardly there seemed to be no time pressure, for we thought we still had the whole of the next semester.

We come now to George's last dream, which he had before starting on his fateful holiday:

> A man—who was either the dreamer himself or his best friend—was to be executed, and the dreamer offered to be the executioner. He did this in the hope of saving the man's life as he believed him to be falsely accused. He had a sharp hunting knife in his hand and had to look as if he were cutting to kill, because if it were discovered that he was trying to save the victim, he would have to pay with his own life. He cut along the lumbar vertebrae and then turned the man over. He heard the bones cracking as he did this and was afraid he had cut too deep. He woke up with the strong feeling—although she is not mentioned directly in the dream—that he would be quite unable to satisfy the girl sexually.

His associations to this dream are very important: the best friend was a man who had been engaged while he was a student to a girl who was an alcoholic. He knew he would be a fool to marry her, broke off the engagement and went back to Europe for several months in order to make the break complete. But when he returned to America, he met her again and married her against light and reason. The marriage was disastrously unhappy. Eventually the wife set fire to her bed while she was drunk and burned to death.

The knife was a cherished possession given to George at the time of his marriage by a very loyal friend. It was so sharp that he could shave with it, but he used it mainly to give the *coup de grâce* while hunting and fishing.

From the association to the best friend—and also from his own irrational feeling about the girl on waking—it seems clear that the dream is insisting on his killing the student in himself who was ever and again trying to solve the problem as if he were still a young man. He knew that even were he still in his first youth he would probably only be repeating the mistake of his first marriage, but again and again he wavered, just as his friend undertook the journey to Europe only to fall into what he knew was a fatal mistake when he returned. The fact that the knife was the one with which he had given many a *coup de grâce* to a wounded deer shows that he must evidently now make up his mind to give the *coup de grâce* to the too youthful man in himself who wants to repeat his earlier mistake. If he does not kill this kind of foolishness, he will forfeit his life. The catastrophic marriage of the friend was the clearest possible warning that nothing but disaster could be expected from a youthful solution. But in the dream he is very half-hearted about it; he evidently really wants to save that young man.

Although the dreamer's own associations all come from the sphere of his personal life, the dream is clearly an individual version of a widespread archetypal motif: the sacrifice of the human ego and unconsciousness for the sake of transformation. This is a central theme of all the great religions, also found all over the world in folklore, primitive rites and so on.

This theme occurs again and again in Jung's *Symbols of Transformation,* where we found many examples with the purpose of enlarging the context and showing George that his dream was not just his personal trouble but a world-wide problem. Moreover, as I pointed out to him, no religion is more concerned with suffering and sacrifice than his own Christianity. Jung speaks, for instance, of sacrifice on a mythological level:

By sacrificing these valued objects of desire and possession, the instinctive desire, or libido, is given up in order that it may be regained in new form. Through sacrifice man ransoms himself from the fear of death and is reconciled to the demands of Hades. In the late cults the hero, who in olden times conquered evil and death through his labours, has become the divine protagonist, the priestly self-sacrificer and renewer of life. Since he is now a divine figure and his sacrifice is a transcendental mystery whose meaning far exceeds the value of an ordinary sacrificial gift, this deepening of the sacrificial symbolism is a reversion to the old idea of human sacrifice, because a stronger and more total expression is needed to portray the idea of *self*-sacrifice. The relation of Mithras to his bull comes very close to this idea. In Christianity it is the hero himself who dies of his own free will.[44]

The sacrifice demanded of George in his dream does not go as far as the total sacrifice demanded here. He is only asked to sacrifice the part of himself that is too young. Moreover, as his association to the knife is using it to kill animals, particularly deer, while hunting, we may assume that the man to be killed is almost an animal. His attitude has remained too young, and unconscious, because physical libido will always remain in, or re-find, the old river beds, unless it is sacrificed again and again. Jung continues:

Even on the primitive level, among the Australian blackfellows, we meet with the idea that the life-force wears out, turns "bad" or gets lost, and must therefore be renewed at regular intervals. Whenever such an *abaissement* occurs the rites of renewal must be performed. There is an infinite number of these rites, but even on a much higher level they retain their original meaning. Thus the Mithraic killing of the bull is a sacrifice to the Terrible Mother, to the unconscious, which spontaneously attracts energy from the conscious mind because it has strayed too far from its roots, forgetting the power of the gods, without whom all life withers or ends catastrophically in a welter of perversity. In the act of sacrifice the consciousness gives up its power and possessions in the interests of the unconscious. This makes possible a union of opposites resulting in a release of energy. At the same time the act of sacrifice is a fertilization of the mother: the chthonic serpent-demon drinks the blood, i.e., the soul, of the hero. In this way life becomes immortal, for, like the sun, the hero regenerates himself by his self-sacrifice and re-entry into the mother. After all this we should have no difficulty in recognizing the son's sacrifice to the mother in the Christian mystery.[45]

---

[44] *Symbols of Transformation,* CW 5, par. 671.
[45] Ibid.

One could say that the friend who should be sacrificed was in love with a perverted image (the young girl who was already a hopeless drunkard). This shows that George's own inner image was perverted—in the literal sense of the word—that is, it had become diverted from the instinctive line, from the Tao, so to speak. Of course his mother complex played a considerable role in the obstinate persistence of his youthful attitude.

Again, Jung:

> Comparison between the Mithraic and the Christian sacrifice should show just where the superiority of the Christian symbol lies: it lies in the frank admission that not only has man's animal instinctuality (symbolized by the bull) to be sacrificed, but the entire natural man, who is more than can be expressed by his theriomorphic symbol. Whereas the latter represents animal instinctuality and utter subjection to the law of the species, the natural man means something more than that, something specifically human, namely the ability to deviate from the law, or what in theological language is known as the capacity for "sin." It is only because this variability in his nature has continually kept other ways open that spiritual development has been possible for *Homo sapiens* at all.[46]

Seen from this angle, it was very meaningful that George's fate had led him into a projected anima situation which was *contra naturam,* against nature. It would have been his great chance to become conscious, but he was still in the phase of his inner development where it was necessary to sacrifice his too youthful point of view and his naive wish to make up at the eleventh hour for all his unlived life.

We see, from this wider context, that this dream also is concerned at bottom with a new attitude to religion, with the same theme as the dreams of the sunken ship and the books. But now the point is being driven much nearer the bone, and the dream is doing just what George was always afraid of in accepting "God's will": revealing the latter as very much opposed to the wishes of the "too young" man in George.

George does indeed realize in the dream that it would be dangerous not to obey the command to kill the young man but he is very ambivalent about it. Jung points out that we find the same split-mindedness in ancient times:

> The head from Ostia [this is the frontispiece to *Symbols of Transformation],* supposed by Cumont to be that of Mithras Tauroctonos, certainly

---

[46] Ibid., par. 673.

wears an expression which we know all too well from our patients as one of sentimental resignation. . . .

Since sentimentality is sister to brutality, and the two are never very far apart, they must be somehow typical of the period between the first and third centuries of our era. The morbid facial expression points to the disunity and split-mindedness of the sacrificer: he wants to, and yet doesn't want to. This conflict tells us that the hero is both the sacrificer and the sacrificed.[47]

George was very sentimental, not only toward the problem of the countertransference girl but also in general. He had real feeling and, as I said before, an unusual love of humanity, but nevertheless, when it came to the point, he was very inclined to escape his problems by a sentimental "I can't hurt anyone" attitude. He found it very difficult to see the hidden brutality which lurked under such banalities, although it was often very obvious to outsiders. It is also obvious in his dream: he wants to save the man's life, even though he realized in the dream that the execution of the man was a higher command which could not be disobeyed.

I gave George a good deal of this interpretation. He accepted it, apparently whole-heartedly as far as the personal aspect went, and said he felt much better for the prospect of a definite plan of action. But that amounted to reasonable resignation and not to sacrifice, and he showed a considerable resistance to the archetypal parallels and to regarding the whole problem from the religious point of view. We hit on the same complex here as had prevented him from facing the problem of rescuing the values from the sunken ship and saving the essence of his theological books. As I pointed out before, this does indeed seem to be the hardest task of all for a theologian. I must admit, however, that though I warned him that if he failed to give the *coup de grâce,* he was likely to miss the whole meaning and value of the rest of his life, in short, his process of individuation. I did not see at the time that this dream meant exactly what it said: if he spared that man, he must forfeit his own life. He died exactly a month after the dream.

I only know a little, from letters, of what happened in that month, for he left Zurich for six weeks' holiday three days after the dream. I had a short letter from him, written a fortnight before his death, in which he said he was enjoying his holiday but would find it very good to get back to Zurich and his analytic work. In his last two weeks, however, he seems to

---

[47] Ibid., pars. 667-668.

have spoken to several people as if he almost expected some disaster, and he also complained that "negative feelings cropped up from time to time." On the other hand, he told one of his near relations that he had now seen what he had longed to see ever since he left Europe as a young man.

We do not know if George's number was up. It is possible that his courageous insight into his personal shadow, rewarded in the last days of his life by seeing something that he had wanted to see since he left Europe thirty-five years before, represented all the renewal he could reach in this life. We can only see that the unconscious speaks a strange, ambiguous language on this subject in his dreams: moving to a distant town, for instance, might mean death, or moving to a totally different attitude in this life. And the beautiful woman, who takes him to a store downtown might be the anima, in her death aspect, who takes him irrevocably to the *Todeshochzeit* in the underworld. Or she might be the living anima who leads him to a hitherto unexperienced life, opening the door to a realm of feeling and eros, rich with new values. Only one dream, the last, is inexorably clear: he must kill the regressive, youthful friend at all costs. This would mean a total sacrifice of childish desire and a new adult attitude toward searching for the meaning of his individual life.

This dream really contains the essence of the change from the first to the second half of life. There are no rules between inner and outer. We cannot know beforehand what should be given up and what retained. The reverse sacrifice, for instance, might have been asked of George: the unconscious might have wanted him to marry the girl, and accept the Hosea-like fate in which that would have involved him.

There seems to be only one rule: the older we get, the less we can afford the infantile foolishness of pampering the ego. We just can't afford to worry any longer about what *"I* want," what *"I* must have" and so on. That way leads inevitably to regression. Meister Eckhart saw this clearly in his teaching of *"sich lassen,"* leaving oneself. He insists again and again that all misery comes from wanting one's personal way. He says, for instance:

> Thou mayest not know it, and it may not seem so to thee, but the only source of restlessness in thee is thy personal will, whether this is realized or not.[48]

We must find out from God what his will is. Broadly speaking, what God

---

[48] *Meister Eckhart,* vol. 2, p. 5.

wills is that we should give up willing. . . . In fact, unless we do give up our will without reserve, we cannot work with God at all.[49]

Meister Eckhart is here stating an empirical, psychological fact in religious language. We can never experience, or work with, the Self—that part of ourselves that does live as if it had centuries to spend—until we have sacrificed the one-sided, short-sighted wishes of our youthful ego, until we have killed this part of ourselves, as George was commanded to kill the too youthful friend in his last dream.

When Meister Eckhart speaks of finding out God's will, psychologically he means the same as Jung meant when he said (in the passage from the E.T.H. lecture which I quoted at the beginning) that self-knowledge does not refer to knowledge of the ego, but to realization of the unknown Self.

In another place Meister Eckhart says:

Remember, in this life no one ever left himself so much but he could find some more to leave. Very few can stand it who know what it really means. It is just a give and take, a mutual exchange: thou goest out of things so much and just so much, no more and no less, does God go in with all of his if thou dost go clean out of all of thine. Try it, though it cost thy all. That way lies true peace and none elsewhere.[50]

As I see it, this was the kernel of the religious attitude that George had to save from the sunken ship. A collective, religious vehicle, which carries us safely earlier in life, may sink and even have to remain at the bottom of the sea, but we cannot ever afford to lose the essence of what it contained. This admittedly involves the difficult task of recognizing "the unknown," of finding out God's will, as Meister Eckhart expresses it, but nevertheless that seems to be the *conditio sine qua non* of renewal in old age.

---

[49] Ibid., p. 16.
[50] Ibid., p. 6.

4
Ego and Shadow

This lecture and the two that follow were originally published by the Guild of Pastoral Psychology in London, England. We know only the dates when these lectures were given, not the circumstances of their presentation. Again, they are vintage Barbara Hannah and illustrate the depth and breadth of her insights into some of Jung's major ideas.

(March 1955)

Although one might think the ego would be the easiest of all Jungian concepts to speak of, I always find it one of, if not the, most difficult. It belongs indeed in the conscious realm—in contrast to other terms such as anima, animus or archetype—but, for that very reason, one finds oneself in the position of Baron Munchhausen who had to pull himself out of the bog by his own plait! One must try to confine oneself to giving a formal description of the ego, for every other way of looking at it would have to allow for *individuality,* which is the main characteristic of every ego. Every ego is different, even unique, so that one can only sketch the main general characteristics very roughly. Any insistence on specifics would do violence to its individual character.

In order to make a start, we will begin with a short summary of Jung's description of the ego in *Aion.* The ego, as a content of consciousness, is a complex of intricate factors. On the one side, it is founded on physical sensations, which are yet perceived psychically from within, and, on the other, on the totality of unconscious psychic contents. These two fields are the foundation of the ego and the ego itself is their point of relation. The ego is presumably brought into existence by the collisions of the body with the environment, and—once a subject is present—goes on developing by collisions with the outer world *and* the inner world. It is individually unique and is the center of the field of consciousness. As such it is the subject of all our efforts at adaptation. On the other hand, it is *not* the center of our personality, although we are often under the illusion that it is.

The common assumption which regards the ego as representing not only the center of our personality but everything that we are, was challenged long before the time of either Freud or Jung. But it is an idea which dies hard, and even today it is a great shock to the average layman when he realizes he is not the master in his own house, that he must reckon with other wills than the one he identifies with in his own field of behavior.

When we study ourselves objectively, we have to realize that the ego is only one among many complexes that exist in our personality,[51] though it is indeed the nuclear center of our field of consciousness. It has a very high degree of continuity and identity, which normally increases in the course of life, but which is also inclined to become more and more one-sided.

As Jung has made particularly clear in his essay, "On the Nature of the Psyche," there is nothing we can really call consciousness on the animal or primitive level, but only a kind of luminosity.[52] Most of us can probably remember a time in our own childhood when our consciousness was on a similar level, when we questioned neither ourselves nor our surroundings, but just accepted things as they were, like an animal. If we look back on those days, we can also remember the emotional moments and incidents that woke us up to a realization of our separate existence.

At first, the experience we gain—in the usually painful way—is like little separated sparks of light in the sea of a general consciousness. Slowly connections appear, resemblances between these experiences, for instance, and gradually these separate sparks cluster together and form a kind of island that we call the ego complex. The ego complex is not, of course, identical with the field of consciousness, which last is more than the function or activity which maintains the relation of the ego with other psychic contents. Everything which is not related to the ego is, for that particular person, unconscious. Consciousness is capable of indefinite extension, whereas the ego complex is more or less bound by the laws of space and time. To use a rather cheap illustration, we might liken the ego to an operator at a telephone exchange, and consciousness to a net of telephone wires all over the world. Obviously this operator can only be con-

---

[51] To define the term "complex" briefly, one might say it is an unconscious or half-conscious cluster of representations laden with emotion. A complex consists of a nucleus and a surrounding field of associations. A complex can be acquired by personal experience, or its nucleus can be formed by an archetypal disposition. The ego complex belongs to the latter category, i.e., it is founded on an archetypal disposition which—by definition—is an unknown psychic fact. We call the ego a complex because it shows all the structural characteristics of other complexes.

[52] *The Structure and Dynamics of the Psyche,* CW 8, par. 387.

nected with one or two wires at the same time, and the ego complex is in much the same position.

Of course, such a simile cannot be ridden to death, for a telephone operator knows where all the wires lead, whereas a great many of the wires which reach the ego come, at times, from an unknown source which, of course, adds greatly to the confusion. But it may serve to illustrate the difference between the ego and the field of consciousness.

Although if we are asked what we mean when we say "I," we usually point to our body, the body is by no means identical with the ego complex. We might almost say that the body is another field of luminosity which is often connected with the ego complex, but which is also frequently separated from it. The intuitive type, for instance, as is well known, is often entirely unaware of the body. It is as if the ego complex, sitting at the telephone exchange, never made use of the wires to the body or—in extreme cases—as if the wires had never been connected. It may even be the main task of an analysis to establish this connection.

In that same essay, "On the Nature of the Psyche," Jung says one could think of psychic processes as a scale along which consciousness "slides":

> At one moment it finds itself in the vicinity of instinct, and falls under its influence; at another, it slides along to the other end where spirit predominates and even assimilates the instinctual processes most opposed to it.[53]

To give a simple example of each end of this scale: A monk, for instance, experiences the archetype of the union of opposites only at the spiritual end of the scale in the idea of the *unio mystica,* whereas a person who is only conscious of the physical end experiences the same archetype in concrete sexuality. Both experience the same living mystery, but one only in the spirit and the other only in the body. Normally, our consciousness is somewhere in between and, therefore, the two experiences are mixed to various degrees.

When consciousness is centered at one end or the other of this scale, we are, of course, particularly prone to be possessed by something which belongs to the other end. We can see this, for instance, in the accounts of St. Anthony and the other ascetic monks, who would sometimes live in the desert for years concentrating upon, and only conscious of, their spirit,

---

[53] Ibid., par. 408.

entirely ignoring their bodies. As is well known, they were tormented by continual visions of naked women and so on, really possessed by their ignored and maltreated bodies. In just the same way, the "isms" are flourishing today mainly on account of the modern materialistic standpoint that ignores the power of the idea.

The ego complex was feeble—one might almost say nonexistent—in primitive man. He required a *rite d'entrée,* something to wake up his emotions, before undertaking any great effort. This always seems a deprived condition to us because in the course of centuries we have developed an amount of free will that is infinitely greater than that of the primitive.

The development of consciousness and the fact that humanity has rescued the ego from the primitive state of twilight sleep are perhaps the greatest achievements of mankind. It is undoubtedly a great mistake to undervalue either the ego or consciousness. Yet we must admit that we live in an age which has grossly overrated their power. In the nineteenth century, it was still possible to believe that they were even powerful enough to bring about a Utopia on earth. But the twentieth century has surely brought us sufficient proof that this was a regrettable error. Therefore, it is certainly wiser to look carefully at the weak points in our consciousness than to trust its strength blindly.

In a seminar given in Zurich in 1935, Jung vividly described the shocks experienced by the ego while it was discovering that it was not the king in its own realm, but only one of many inhabitants in a vast, mainly unexplored land, ruled over by an "unknown grand power."[54] This grand power would represent the Self, as we know it in Jungian psychology.

It is clear that the ego is by no means absolved from responsibility for its own small corner of the psyche by the existence of this "unknown grand power," and also that the ego is really in a much weaker position while it is unaware of this power than when it accepts its rule and tries to come to terms with it.

It is also evident that the small island of the ego complex has always had difficulty in maintaining itself in the great sea of the unconscious, and that therefore it is only to be expected that every ego complex will have an innate tendency to build itself ramparts, as it were, as a defense against invasion from within and without. On the inner side, this defense is a

---

[54] See *Nietzsche's* Zarathustra: *Notes of the Seminar Given in 1934-1939,* vol. 1, pp. 390f.

natural phenomenon and is formed by animus and anima. Anima is the Jungian term for the feminine soul of man, and animus the term for the masculine spirit of woman. These complexes have an individual character so that, when we investigate them, we find ourselves justified in speaking of "my" animus or "your" anima. But, on the other hand, they are figures of the collective unconscious and thus form a kind of natural barrier between the individual and collective territories.

Although the real function of animus and anima is to protect the ego and to bring unintegrated contents of the unconscious to its notice, both these figures—particularly before we recognize them and come to terms with them—are apt to affect the ego in a most unpleasant way. The anima produces disturbing moods in a man, and the animus rigid opinions in a woman. In general, they act as a sort of rampart against the waves of the unconscious, but the moods and opinions are a great difficulty when we are trying to see behind them and to reduce anima and animus to their proper place in our psyche as mediators between conscious and unconscious. However, even in their negative aspect they have their positive use and, undoubtedly, they often protect a too-weak consciousness from the waves of the unknown which might overwhelm it.

Persona

Facing the outer world, the rampart is formed by the so-called persona, which is the Latin word for an actor's mask. Its original function was to signify the role played by an actor, and thus the very word contains a certain suggestion of "putting on an act," or "playing to the gallery," that is, appearing as something which is just *not* what we really are.

It would be a great mistake to think of the persona as a conscious deception. It is something that forms quite naturally from our childhood on, and people often find it almost as difficult to see their persona as to become aware of their shadow, animus or anima. The persona usually begins to form as a result of conflict with the outer environment. The complete naturalness of a child, for instance, is apt to be embarrassing to the adults around them, and most children learn fairly early to protect themselves by hiding their most spontaneous reactions. They often see, for instance, that some child in their environment gets on better in this respect, does not put his or her foot into it so regularly, and almost unconsciously they pick up something from that child. Or they admire somebody they know and, consciously or unconsciously, begin to imitate them. Or they realize that some natural characteristic of their own makes an impression and they begin to use it for that purpose instead of spontaneously, and so on.

That the persona is the result of contact with the environment is shown by the fact that if people are alone for a long time, they lose their personas. I remember seeing the photograph of a man who had gone to the Arctic regions for observations. He got caught in an avalanche and was completely buried by the snow, which also covered the high pole he had set up as a landmark, so the relief party failed to find him. He had been buried for several months and without light for six weeks. All trace of any masculine persona was gone and he looked exactly like a woman. No doubt, as he returned to civilization, his persona built up again, but for a time there was no trace of it. A similar change has been noticed by other people who have met their friends coming from long periods of isolation.

The development of the persona forms an important part in education. You can see this particularly clearly in the English public schools, where it is—or, at any rate, was in my generation—far more important to become a "gentleman" than to pass examinations with credit. The boy who will not take on the "old school tie" ideal is, or was, more or less an outcast from the beginning. I saw this clearly with my own three brothers. The two younger ones took over the public school persona without difficulty and thus fitted into their environment easily. But my eldest brother just could not accept it. Consequently he was miserable at his school, and always gave the impression of being an oversensitive snail who had somehow mislaid its shell. After several years of being a lecturer, he acquired a peculiar kind of ill-fitting, professorial persona which he always produced at the wrong moment. He would suddenly address a luncheon party, for instance, as if it were a class of small boys. He was well over fifty before he overcame the disadvantages of his early experience.

Naturally, when we grow up and have to adapt and even earn our living by means of the way we can fit ourselves into our environment, the building up of a suitable persona becomes vitally important, but how it goes on strengthening is much the same as in childhood. It consists really of tiny fragments which slowly amalgamate to form a kind of crust between the ego complex and the outside world. For the most part, these fragments come from general collective values, from behaviors that are acceptable to the general public and are adapted to the social values of our time. The individual nature is mainly to be found in the particular *choice* of this or that element, so one can say that the persona is partly the effect of what our environment obliges us to be, that is, totally impersonal, and partly oneself, personal. This structure resembles that of its inner counterpart, the anima or animus, which also has individual and collective aspects.

It is evident that a persona is an indispensable part of the personality. People with a deficient persona are really at a great disadvantage in outer life. They have no shield against the projections of others and are in constant danger of falling back into the original state of *participation mystique* with their environment.

Its dangers, however, are equally apparent. As we have seen, it is a mask, a role, seldom the true essence of our personality, and we are always in peril of identifying with it. In the first half of life, we must indeed identify with it to some considerable extent or we shall not succeed in meeting the demands of our profession or of life. But in the second half of life, because it only contains a small fraction of what we really are, identification with it becomes a great hindrance, especially if we have used it, as is only too often the case, as a mask toward ourselves as well as toward others. Everyone knows examples of people who believe implicitly that they are what they appear to be—and how empty and shallow they become. I remember once, when I was leaving the old Roman theater at Carthage, where we had seen a rather poor French rendering of a Greek play. I saw one of the actors, unable to relinquish his role, acting it all over again by himself behind an old Roman wall. I cannot tell you how ridiculous he looked, and yet I have often involuntarily been reminded of him as I have watched older people who have remained identical with their persona.

It would of course be exceedingly inconsiderate and unwise to throw away our persona as we become older. It would be like throwing away our clothes and appearing naked in public. There is a story of the poet Shelley that illustrates this point quite well. His father had an estate in Sussex, where there was a pond large enough for swimming. Shelley was very fond of the water and spent a lot of time there. One day he suddenly remembered that it must be past lunch time and, forgetting everything but his stomach, hurried off to the dining room, appearing before a conventional Sussex lunch party without a stitch of clothing. When he saw their horrified faces, he still did not tumble to the real situation and said in surprise: "Why, it is only me"! Although it may not be so evident, "only me" has quite as disturbing an effect in the psychic as it does in the physical sense.

We must have a persona, then, just as we must have clothes, but we must gradually learn to use it rather the same way as we use our clothes. This is by no means as easy as it sounds, for in many cases the persona has grown into our flesh, so to speak, and is no longer detachable. There is, then, only one thing we can do: realize that every solid object on this earth casts a shadow and turn round and face this fact. If we are at all honest in this attempt, we shall soon realize that there are many things which are undeniably part of ourselves, but which do not fit at all with our idea of ourselves or our persona. The realization of these factors will provide us with all the material we need in order to detach ourselves from identification with the persona.

Shadow

As we try to adapt ourselves to the outer world and begin to form our persona, we mostly tend to repress those qualities that hinder us in this task, or that spoil the ideal picture of ourselves that we secretly cherish. These qualities retire into the dark, often highly charged with emotion, but they continue to exist and are usually a good deal more visible to our neighbors than they are to ourselves.

Undeniably it is a terrifying undertaking, and one that must be faced again and again, to turn our backs on familiar illusions concerning our own character and face the unknown darkness behind. It is indeed, as Jung once said, an almost superhuman task. But every sincere effort in this direction, however small, is the one task which never lets us down. Whatever ground we can reclaim from the shadow is firm and fertile ground that enables us to commence building the house founded on the rock. In contrast, everything built only on the light side of the ego complex or on the persona, invariably turns out to have been built on sand.

It is a platitude to point out that everything in this world consists at bottom of an equal amount of black and white, of light and darkness, and yet, when it comes to ourselves, we easily lose sight of this fact, obvious and simple as it is. Moreover, we find it all but impossible to see our dark side without losing confidence in our light side. Yet this is indispensable, for, naturally, the fact that we also have shadow qualities in no way cancels out our good qualities. Actually, it is never so necessary to keep them in mind as when we are facing the fact that we have repressed a great deal which is their direct opposite.[55]

Although it is painful and humiliating to face our less admirable qualities, it would be comparatively easy were it not for the fact that everything
which falls into the unconscious becomes contaminated with other contents. To give one example: the personal shadow becomes contaminated
with the collective shadow. The word "collective," as it is used in Jungian
psychology, applies to all psychic contents which are not peculiar to one
individual, but common to many at the same time, that is, to a society, a
people or to mankind in general. The personal unconscious, therefore, consists of contents which belong to that one person, and the collective unconscious of contents which are common to many or even all. Insofar as
we are aware of our personal shadow, it is attached to our ego like the actual shadow to our body. But, insofar as we are not aware of it, it falls into
the unconscious and becomes indistinguishable from the other contents of
the unconscious, particularly from the collective shadow. Then people can
even fall into the error of regarding their personal shadow as the devil himself. This is perhaps the most difficult aspect of the shadow problem, but I
hope to make it somewhat clearer later, by means of a dream.

The second great difficulty in recognizing the shadow is due to the fact
that all the things we lose sight of in ourselves have a tendency to be projected onto our outer environment. Of course, we never consciously *make*
projections, but there is some unconscious factor in us which seems to
have a devilish habit of slipping these repressed pieces of our own personality into someone else. (Naturally there is some similarity, or there would
be no hook for the projection.) I remind the reader, for instance, of the
many people who cherish a *bête noir*. This *bête noir* usually carries the
projection of what we hate most in ourselves, and it is also just this projection which falsifies our picture of the person in question, making him
or her so completely unacceptable.

It is a very difficult task to disentangle such a projected factor from the
carrier of the projection. Perhaps one of the most dependable indicators of a
projection is the presence of emotion. If other people's weaknesses or bad
qualities make us unduly angry, we may be pretty sure there is some pro-

---

[55] As Shakespeare says: "The web of our life is of a mingled yarn, good and ill
together: our virtues would be proud, if our faults whipped them not, and our
crimes would despair, if they were not cherished by our virtues." *(All's Well
That Ends Well*, act 4, scene 3)

jection involved, because at bottom we do not resent the weaknesses of others—they may even give us a pleasant feeling of superiority. *The weakness or bad qualities that we resent are always our own.* There is, of course, always the danger of introjecting such qualities if this point of view is exaggerated, that is, of taking into ourselves traits that do not belong to us. But we have a certain instinctive recognition of what does or does not belong to us, an instinct which only fails us if we do not want to see ourselves as we really are. This instinct says, "It clicks," when something returns that is really ourselves, and says "No" when we try to introject. Whether "it clicks" or not is really our final criterion.

Another way we can realize our shadow is by our effect on the people around us, for we do have certain effects on other people that we can neither predict nor adequately explain. To give an extreme example: we had a washerwoman when I was a child who always quarreled with everyone in her environment. When rebuked for this fault, full of injured innocence, she replied, "How can I help that? I never saw anything like the tempers in the people I meet!" Of course, in such a case it is not difficult—though undoubtedly painful—to see that the temper is our own. But it becomes much more difficult when the effect comes from something far more obscure than a bad temper. The mechanism, however, is always the same and, when we continually have the same effect on different people, it is a place where we are likely to make valuable discoveries about our shadow, animus or anima.

Perhaps it should just be mentioned here that, naturally, an unknown shadow does not only get contaminated in the unconscious with the collective shadow, but also with other dominants, most particularly with anima and animus. This often results in a kind of marriage between shadow and animus or anima, which is particularly disastrous to the ego, for it is then at a disadvantage with the unconscious, being outnumbered.

In the 1935 seminar mentioned earlier, Jung gave a description of accepting the shadow that has always remained in my mind.[56] Briefly, he used the simile of our consciousness being like a ship or bowl floating on the surface of the unconscious. Each part of the shadow that we realize has a weight, and our consciousness is lowered to that extent when we take it into our boat. Therefore, we might say that the main art of dealing with

---

[56] *Nietzsche's* Zarathustra, vol. 1, pp. 478f.

the shadow consists in the right loading of our boat: if we take on too little, we float right away from reality and become like a fluffy white cloud in the sky. If we take on too much, we may sink our boat.

We must still ask ourselves the question, what does a lowered consciousness mean practically? This is very difficult to answer theoretically, as it is really a matter of experience. Consciousness is mainly connected with our superior functions, where we are capable of a very clear, though one-sided, conscious perception. But, when we bring up something from the unconscious which demands a broader reaction, it forces us to widen our point of view, because we must then also react with our undeveloped functions and our instinctive side. We are thus confronted with the task of reconciling the reactions of our clear consciousness with those from the darkness or, at best, from the dim luminosity of our inferior or instinctive side. This naturally dims or lowers consciousness, but at the same time it makes it more substantial, three-dimensional instead of two-dimensional, so to speak.

There is another important aspect of the shadow which we must mention. Many people live the negative side of themselves, and then the shadow can be much more decent and have more positive qualities than the conscious ego. You all know the sort of people who live their shadow, as it were: they are always putting the wrong foot forward, and sometimes even seem to indulge in such behavior. If you ask such people about their shadow, they will inform you that it is terrible, a cut-throat, a murderer, and so on, because of the general illusion that the shadow must be negative. But if this film of illusion can be removed, one often discovers a most decent person behind it. Jung even said once in a seminar that there can be eighty percent pure gold in the shadow.

The great difficult in discovering the shadow is to find—or perhaps still more to acknowledge—*just the components* of which it is made. Naturally, it is pleasanter to find gold than a decaying corpse, for instance, and preferable to discover that we are more decent than we thought rather than vice versa. But, curiously enough, it is often just the people with the pure gold in their shadow who show the most resistance to digging it out. This is usually because they had a secret purpose, perhaps unknown to themselves, in burying the gold or repressing their positive characteristics. Good qualities carry an obligation, and possibly they did not want to take the responsibility which is always involved when we live something positive. Such people are like the man in Christ's parable who preferred to bury his talent; in other words, they live below their real level in order to shirk the responsibility of what they could be.

To sum up the relation of ego and personal shadow as simply as possible, one could say that the one is always the reverse of the other and that, therefore, discovering one's one shadow is necessarily pioneer work. The exact elements of which it is composed are different in every case and general rules are usually more misleading than helpful.

Robert Louis Stevenson's Dream

In order to illustrate the foregoing, I have chosen a dream of Stevenson's which was the foundation of his famous story, *Dr. Jekyll and Mr. Hyde*. The problem of ego and shadow is extraordinarily frequent in Stevenson's books, but we have only time to consider this one fragment.

The unconscious played an enormous role in Stevenson's writing. He says himself that his Brownies "do one half of all my work for me while I am fast asleep, and in all human likelihood, do the rest for me as well, when I am wide awake and fondly suppose I do it for myself."[57] He presents a lot of evidence in "A Chapter on Dreams" in *Across the Plains*. In this chapter he tells us that he had long been trying to find a vehicle for "the strong sense of man's double being which must at times come in upon and overwhelm the mind of every thinking creature,"[58] when he had a dream which laid the foundation for *Dr. Jekyll and Mr. Hyde*.

The dream he had was the "scene at the window" which, considerably condensed, runs as follows:

Mr. Utterson, the lawyer, who is the observer in the book and collects the material, was taking his usual Sunday walk with his kinsman, Mr. Richard Enfield, a well-known man about town. They walked into the court of Dr. Jekyll's house and saw the latter sitting at a window, looking infinitely sad. He refused to join their walk, but expressed pleasure at the idea of a short talk from the window. He had hardly spoken before the smile was struck from of his face and succeeded by an expression of such abject terror and despair as froze the very blood of the two gentlemen below. Dr. Jekyll instantly closed the window and the two men, pale and horrified, left the court, with Mr. Utterson muttering the rather surprising

---

[57] *Across the Plains,* p. 225.
[58] Ibid., p. 227.

words: "God forgive us, God forgive us," to which Mr. Enfield very seriously assented.

Stevenson's dream continued with another scene, in which Mr. Hyde, pursued for some other crime, took the powder and underwent the change (into Dr. Jekyll) in the presence of his pursuers. The scene at the window was taken into the book as it was, though probably the names were a conscious elaboration. The second scene, on the other hand, was not taken over quite as it was dreamed, but became the theme of the whole story.

We have no space to deal with the story as Stevenson wrote it. It is extremely well known, but I will just remind the reader that it deals with the particularly worthy, benevolent and philanthropic Dr. Jekyll. He invents a powder enabling him to turn into his own opposite, and thus to enjoy the pleasures that he was unable "to reconcile with his imperious desire to carry his head high and wear a more than commonly grave countenance before the public."[59] At first his pleasures were merely worldly and undignified, but Mr. Hyde became more and more completely evil and eventually did not stop even at murder. The change, which at first was entirely voluntary, also became uncontrollable. By the end, the personality of Dr. Jekyll becomes entirely submerged in Mr. Hyde.

When Stevenson was a student, he was very seriously threatened by his terrible dreams—examples can be found in the "Chapter on Dreams"—but a doctor was able to put a stop to them for a while. Later, Stevenson himself hit on the method of using them in his literary work. His so-called Brownies cooperated in this work, and he was able to channel his consciousness into his creative work in a way that has much to recommend it. One knows, indeed, the excellent therapeutic effect which creative work can have, and for Stephenson, in his time and circumstances, it was probably the only solution, to say nothing of the great interest of several of his stories from the psychological point of view and leaving aside the question of literary merit. If I discuss his dream as if it were brought by a patient in analysis, it must be understood that I mean no criticism of Stevenson. It is hardly necessary to mention also that I try to understand the dream as it applies to our theme, and that it would depend on a great many circumstances how much or how little should be told to the dreamer himself.

To me, the most striking feature in the dream—apart from the dramatic

---

[59] *Dr. Jekyll and Mr. Hyde*, p. 78.

change from Hyde to Jekyll and the terrific emotional content in the anguish of Dr. Jekyll at the window, reflected in the two onlookers—is the fact that there are four male figures—the number of the totality—and no woman. In the book, also, there is no significant anima figure. (She only makes an important appearance in her negative aspect as Mr. Hyde's evil landlady.) Stevenson was an only child with a strong mother complex which he never outgrew. He married, indeed, but his wife was very much older than himself, with two children from an earlier marriage. In their subsequent life in various places all over the world, Stevenson always seems to have been more the eldest son than the husband. It is clear, therefore, that his problem would more likely be concerned with the shadow, that is, with finding his own masculinity, than with the anima.

Therefore, if we consider this dream from the standpoint of Stevenson's own psychology, I think we should be justified in assuming that the figure of Mr. Utterson, the lawyer and onlooker in the drama, represents the ego. He gives one the impression of being the narrator of the story, though the book is not actually written in the first person. Much of the fatal outcome might have been avoided had Mr. Utterson been aware of the facts before the end of the drama; this was a change for the worse made by Stevenson, for in the dream Utterson knew the secret. Mr. Enfield, the man about town, would more or less represent the personal shadow, with a wordly point of view, a side which Stevenson lived very little.

The other two figures that appear in the dream, Dr. Jekyll and Mr. Hyde, have a more collective or larger-than-life character. The fact that one can turn into the other by means of a powder stamps them as inhuman, for such a metamorphosis is something beyond human capacity. This hypothesis is also hinted at in the dream by the fact that Dr. Jekyll only talks to the two men from an upper window. Moreover, it is confirmed in the book, for neither Jekyll nor Hyde are really human beings: the latter particularly represents the principle of evil per se and is far more an archetypal figure belonging to the collective unconscious than anything like a personal shadow. If, therefore, we were confronted with this dream in a modern individual, the first and most important thing to do would be to separate the personal from the superpersonal or collective elements, and to insist on the fact that Utterson and Enfield were the first concern of the dreamer, because they more or less represent the human sphere where the dreamer can do something about it.

Mr. Utterson's strange words as he walks away with Mr. Enfield—"God forgive us, God forgive us"—throw an interesting light on the problem. Apparently Dr. Jekyll's anguish was no fault of either Utterson or Enfield. But we must not forget that the dream goes on with the transformation scene, so that Stevenson, when he woke from it, knew what Jekyll's anguish was about. Therefore, we cannot escape the conclusion that Stevenson's dream represents the human pair in some way guilty for the anguish of Dr. Jekyll and the crime of Mr. Hyde, or why should Utterson ask God to forgive them, with the full assent of Mr. Enfield?

We know that at the time Stevenson had the dream, he was deeply concerned with a strong sense of man's double being, and that he regarded this as the "hard law of life which lies at the root of religion and is one of the most plentiful springs of distress."[60] The only place that Stevenson could have met this double being in himself is depicted in the dream by the two men who more or less represent what we call ego and shadow. But when the ego tries to have it out with the shadow, it is a problem that inevitably leads to the utmost suffering. Man is crucified, so to speak, between the opposite tendencies in himself, between his virtues and his vices. And it is just this suffering that the two men wanted to escape: the one, Utterson, by keeping out of life himself and being only an onlooker at the game, and the other, Enfield, by being "a man about town," drowning all serious considerations by social diversions.

This theme of escaping suffering is underlined in the book Stevenson wrote from the dream. The purpose of the transforming powder is to free the upright and the unjust twins in human nature from each other, so that the one might pursue virtue and the other vice. Unchecked by the other, one is no longer exposed to disgrace, and the other can go his evil way unhindered by the remorse of his virtuous brother.

We can see something of the same process at work in Stevenson's own life. He came from a family of lighthouse engineers and was originally destined for this career. His grandfather, the famous Robert Stevenson, conquered the dangerous Bell Rock in Scotland to the fury of Scottish smugglers. Perfection was the elder Stevenson's design, and his grandson was brought up in the same ideal. Our author's mother was a minister's daughter and, with all this virtue and light in the family, it is no wonder

---

[60] Ibid., p. 79.

that Louis—like his own Dr. Jekyll—could not bear the flaws in his own character. He was a typical *puer aeternus,* flying high above reality and forever running away from circumstances that would have forced him to face himself as he was. From the time he left his parent's house in Edinburgh in his early twenties, he was always on the move until he built his house in Samoa, in very exotic conditions, some three years before his death at the age of forty-three. The solitary exception was two and a half years in a house at Bournemouth, given to his wife by her father. Here he wrote *Dr. Jekyll and Mr. Hyde.*

The point I want to make is that when a man realizes his dual nature—as Stevenson certainly did—the problem of good and evil has irrevocably been constellated in him. He then has the choice of consciously taking up this problem with his personal shadow in the human realm, or repressing it. In the latter case, it will still take place but in the unconscious, entirely beyond his control, out of sight, glimpsed only occasionally in a dream.

Stevenson depicts this psychological fact very clearly in the story. At the beginning, Dr. Jekyll's only fault is a certain impatient gaiety of disposition, and his pleasures are merely undignified. But when he rids himself of these flaws in his dignified person and drinks the powder to escape suffering from them—in other words, when he rejects the personal shadow—Mr. Hyde becomes purely evil, a murderer and a monster, from whom all men flee. In other words, the rejected personal shadow has become contaminated with the principle of evil and has practically become the devil himself.

Perhaps now we can understand why, in Stevenson's dream, Mr. Utterson asks God to forgive him and Mr. Enfield for the anguish of Dr. Jekyll. Looked at superficially, they are not responsible; yet, if the problem of man's dual nature had been met on the human level, it would never have been pushed into the unconscious, where it can only take place in a kind of archetypal drama, such as the story of Jekyll and Hyde.

The dual figure appears in the dream first as the anguished Dr. Jekyll. In the next scene, it appears as Mr. Hyde, pursued for a crime, who then swallows the powder and changes into Jekyll in the presence of his pursuers. The most striking point here, for a modern dreamer, would be the fact that these two superpersonal figures—the one the prototype of philanthropy and uprightness and the other of crime—are one and the same. Those who have read Jung's "Answer to Job" or Dr. Rivkah Scharf's *Satan in the Old Testament,* are already accustomed to the idea that even God, as a union of opposites, contains good and evil in equal measure. We find the same phenomenon in many archetypal figures as they appear in myth and fairy tale. Stevenson's dream is another grain of evidence which points in the same direction.

It is interesting that the transformation in the dream is from Hyde to Jekyll, whereas in the book the change from Jekyll to Hyde is emphasized. Not only is it Jekyll who makes the powder and originally changes into Hyde, but at the end, Jekyll turns into Hyde involuntarily and—when the original powder is exhausted—can no longer regain the Jekyll shape at all. Moreover, in the dream the change takes place in the public eye, a motif that was only taken into the book in a very modified form, the change always taking place in secret, except once, when Hyde changed into Jekyll before the horrified eyes of a physician, Dr. Lanyon.

In the dream, however, the secret is revealed before the eyes of Hyde's pursuers in an attempt to save himself from the results of his crime. It happens on the superpersonal level, but the thoughtful modern dreamer would have to ask whether there was not something pretty evil taking refuge behind the façade of an ultrarespectable persona that it would be wise to investigate. If the dreamer could heed the warning in such a dream, it might still be solved on a personal level. If the warning were repressed, the personal shadow, capable of crime, would escape into the unconscious where it would become contaminated by collective evil and eventually contribute to a catastrophe that would be visible to all.

In this connection, I should like to quote a short extract from Jung's essay, "The Fight with the Shadow." He is speaking of the Swiss having decided to avoid external wars, thus taking the strife back into their own country, where their warlike instincts spend themselves in the form of domestic quarrels called "political life." He says:

> Yet even our national, mitigated state of war would come to an end if everybody could see his own shadow and begin the only struggle that is really worth while: the fight against the overwhelming power-drive of the shadow. We have a tolerable social order in Switzerland because we fight among ourselves. Our order would be perfect if only everybody could direct his aggressiveness inwards into his own psyche.[61]

---

[61] *Civilization in Transition,* CW 10, par. 455.

As I see it, therefore, the ultimate meaning of Stevenson's dream is to awaken the concern of the individual to this "only struggle that is really worth while," the struggle between ego and shadow. But then comes the most difficult question of all: what should be the practical outcome of such a dream? For instance, should Utterson, as the representative of the ego, leave his detached attitude to life and give himself over to his Enfield shadow and the pleasures which a "man about town" can enjoy? Or should he try to change Enfield?

The first alternative suggests a very common misunderstanding, namely that accepting the shadow simply means living out one's shadow qualities. People behave in the most meaningless irrelevant way and then say, as if that explained the matter completely: "Oh, I am just living my shadow." The second alternative is seldom successful, for the shadow rarely lends itself to change.

Occasionally such a dream may indeed be enough to shock both ego and shadow into a voluntary change. If the realization that they were to blame, expressed in the words, "God forgive us," were deep enough, Utterson would naturally give up something of his detached attitude and Enfield would no longer be satisfied with his "man about town" life. In other words, both would accept a certain uncertainty about their hitherto one-sided attitude.

Accepting uncertainty is perhaps the key which comes nearest to unlocking the door of the problem between ego and shadow. Had Stevenson been in a position to understand his dream subjectively, that is, to regard the people in it as figures in his own psyche, he might have put this theory into practice. We know from his own words that he had "a strong sense of man's double being," which is a "plentiful source of suffering" and "the hard fact that lies at the bottom of religion." But he did not draw the conclusion that this means living with and enduring a constant doubt about oneself. To accept the shadow, as I mentioned before, is to be crucified between one's virtues and one's vices, never sure which has to be lived, for only after one has suffered the utmost conflict between the two can a "third" be born which is neither the one nor the other, but something which comes closer to the totality of human nature.

Accepting the shadow, although it lowers one's boat and smashes one's optimistic illusions, is by no means a loss. I should like to conclude by quoting a few words from Jung's essay, "After the Catastrophe":

If only people could realize what an enrichment it is to find one's own guilt, what a sense of honour and spiritual dignity! But nowhere does there seem to be a glimmering of this insight. Instead, we hear only of attempts to shift the blame on to others.[62]

---

[62] Ibid., par. 416.

5
The Religious Function of the Animus
in the Book of Tobit

(October 7, 1960)

After the title of my lecture was already announced, I realized it might be misleading as to the nature of the material we are to deal with. The Book of Tobit is a very old document (about the third century B.C.) and it is certainly based on still older (Egyptian or Persian) sources.[63] All such books—which have passed through a great many hands— have to be considered as we do myths and fairy tales; that is, they can usually be taken from both the masculine and the feminine side. Therefore, this story could just as well, and perhaps better, be taken as representing masculine psychology, in which case Sarah would be the demon-possessed anima, instead of an animus-possessed girl.

The reason I have used this story in my seminars on feminine psychology is that it is the prototype of demon possession par excellence. It is quoted again and again in medieval material, always in connection with a possessed girl, and it certainly also makes sense from this angle, as I hope we shall see.

As I have to condense a seminar which took seven double hours into an hour, I shall only be able to address the main points and pass over a great deal of importance and interest. For instance, regarding the history of the Book of Tobit, I can only refer you to the excellent introduction in the Oxford University edition of "The Apocrypha and Pseudoepigrapha of the Old Testament" (1913, volume 1). Simpson, the editor of the text, offers convincing proof that the book was written by an exiled Jew in Egypt, but this is a controversial point among scholars, many favoring a Persian, Zoroastrian background.

---

[63] [The Book of Tobit is one of the books of the Old Testament Apocrypha. Although it is not found in most Protestant or Jewish Bibles, it is readily available in Catholic Bibles and, for instance, The New Jerusalem Bible and the Revised Standard Version. The specific source for the various passages cited in this talk are not known, but they do not vary greatly from the Oxford University Press edition noted here in the Bibliography.—Ed.]

I must make it clear from the beginning, however, that Sarah's possession by Asmodaeus is by no means a case of possession by an individual animus. We cannot regard this story from the point of view of personal psychology at all. Rather it has the value of a paradigm, a prototype or pattern, an anticipation of the far later development of the animus in feminine psychology and the individual anima in masculine. It shows us the archetypal background, the foundation on which every individual case of the kind is based. It is the story of a girl possessed by a male demon and her recovery, which certainly dates long before the Book of Tobit, and which reappears in myths and fairy tales all over the world. It is a possession by an extraneous demon, Asmodaeus. The Encyclopedia Britannica says of Asmodaeus that he was "an evil demon who appears in later Jewish traditions as the 'king of demons.' " He is thus a parallel to the Christian devil and represented a very exaggerated case of animus possession. But it is just in the exaggerated case that one can see the mechanism clearly, which helps one to recognize the phenomenon in the more personal case.

One should perhaps mention that the story is mainly concerned with a renewal of consciousness that is, on the one side, too narrow—bound in tradition—and, on the other, too wide, as the unconscious personality is inflated, that is, possessed by an archetypal figure.

The book begins with two parallel stories, that of Tobit and his son Tobias, and of Sarah and her father Raguel. Although they are very near relatives, they are completely separated at the beginning of the book, with no outer communication between the two houses. Nevertheless there is an extraordinary synchronicity at first in the experiences of the old Tobit and the young Sarah.

Tobit represents tradition. His previous history was a story of exile, of stolen visits to Jerusalem and a determination to bury every one of his own race—he was a Jew—who was found murdered or dead. He was always being persecuted for this activity; he had to fly for his life and lost all his possessions but, immediately on his return, he did it again.

We see here a good example of a traditional consciousness that has become too narrow. Tobit was only concerned with burying the dead; he had no idea of the eternal truth of Christ's later saying: "Follow me; and let the dead bury their dead."[64]

---

[64] Matt. 8:22, King James Version.

But, as no persecution turned Tobit from his preoccupation with the past, nature itself took a hand in the game. He lay down in the courtyard—exhausted by one of the dangerous burials—and the droppings of sparrows fell into his eyes and blinded him completely.

It is interesting that sparrows are the birds of Aphrodite and of other love goddesses in the Near East. Aphrodite has a heavenly aspect, symbolized by her well-known bird, the dove, and a common earthly aspect, symbolized by the sparrow. It is striking that it was just the birds of the goddess of love that blinded Tobit and put a stop to his outer sterile activity.

Tobit himself was unable to do anything with the new material presented to him by the sparrows. Thwarted in his usual activities, he had a serious quarrel with his wife Anna, falsely accusing her of stealing a kid, and she—goaded beyond all wifely submission—said: "Where are thine alms-deeds? Where is thy righteous course of life? Behold, this thy case is known."

This was altogether too much for Tobit and he prayed that he might die, "for it is more profitable for me to die than to live, because I have heard false reproaches and there is much sorrow in me." This is really a summit of projection: he has falsely accused his wife, and then complained that "false reproaches" were being made to him. We see very clearly here that the consciousness represented by Tobit is in most urgent need of renewal.

On the very same day his future daughter-in-law, Sarah, far away in Media, was fundamentally in the same trouble. Sarah had been married to seven husbands, all of whom had been killed on the wedding night, before the consummation of the marriage, by the demon Asmodaeus, who was bound in her body. Just as it was the common little sparrows that put an end to Tobit's burying of the dead, so it was now one of her father's maid-servants that put a stop to Sarah's career as a husband killer. She reproached Sarah very roundly, saying: "It is *thou* that slayest thy husbands," and went on to say that her conduct was "scourging" the whole household. Now Sarah had no more use for reproaches than Tobit, but they had their effect. She went up into her father's room and "desired to hang herself." But she decided against doing so because they would then reproach her father, and she would thus bring her "father's old age with sorrow to Hades." So she also—at exactly the same time as Tobit—prayed for death that she might "no more hear reproaches."

The connection between the two is very striking, whether we take Sarah as the prototype of the animus-possessed girl and Tobit as the traditional opinionated mind, or Tobit as the prototype of man whose stupidity and narrow-mindedness has delivered his anima into a state of devil possession. It works both ways:

1) If man's logos is out of order—an extreme example would be a Nazi or Communist mentality—woman's eros is disturbed or even ruined.

2) If a woman's eros is out of order—an extreme example is Sarah, who has killed seven husbands—man's logos is disturbed or even ruined.

3) Anima eros in man destroys woman's logos.

4) Animus logos in woman destroys man's eros.

Neither man nor woman can be destroyed—or destroy him- or herself—without ruining the other. This applies both to their anima and animus, but also to every deeper relationship between the sexes. A time is thus described in the condition of Tobit and Sarah that has a strong resemblance to our own, where we also are faced with the alternative of gaining a completely new consciousness or risking utter destruction.

The fact that neither Tobit nor Sarah can bear reproaches belongs partly to the time and possibly to the Egyptian origin. I remind you of the negative confession in the "Book of the Dead" where the dead mention all possible sins with the assertions that they have *not* committed them. The more primitive a people, the more terror in admitting that they have transgressed the law. And recent events do not justify much optimism that we are any less primitive in this respect.

Apparently both old Tobit and young Sarah had reached the limit of their endurance, for we read next: "At the self-same time the prayer of both was heard before the glory of God." God decided to help them and the archangel Raphael "was sent to heal them both," Tobit of his blindness that he might "see the light of God," and Sarah of her possession by "Asmodaeus, the evil demon." The latter was to be unbound from her so that she might become a fit wife for Tobias, Tobit's son.

God—having heard their prayer—put the matter into exalted hands, but then Asmodaeus is an exalted demon, if one can say such a thing. I have no time to prove this to you, but you can find the material in Simpson's introduction to the Book of Tobit. So God, when He once woke up to the situation, sent a highly positive figure to earth who would be at least an equal counterpart of the negative one in possession.

It strikes me as very interesting that it is the dark side, Asmodaeus, that is in complete possession at the beginning of the story. This agrees with our own experience of the animus: he is usually met with first in his negative aspect, as an opinionating and destructive demon. It is only when the woman has realized this—as the maid-servant obliged Sarah to realize it—and accepted the suffering it has brought to herself and to others, that what one may call the religious function of the animus can come into being. Sarah prayed to God in her extremity; in psychological language, she turned to the Self, the totality, thus admitting the impotence of the ego to find a solution. God heard her, and the divine part of the psyche, in its most positive aspect, came into play. It is interesting too that it is only when *both* Tobit and Sarah have reached the limit of their endurance that the positive side is constellated.

Sarah then is to be freed of her possession and Tobit is to see "the light of God." Only a completely new consciousness—described here as the light of God—can cure Tobit's blind stupidity. On the one side, eros is to be released, and on the other, logos, so that a totally new *coniunctio* may be possible, symbolized here as a marriage between Tobias and Sarah.

Just as Tobit and Sarah prayed at the self-same time and were heard together, now we hear that directly after their prayer, they each changed their locality. He came *in* from the courtyard; that is, thwarted by the sparrows in his regressive outward activities, he turned inward. And Sarah came *down* from her father's upper room; that is, she moved out of her father complex—which always has the effect of keeping the woman too high up, as the Princess in the Ivory Tower, so to speak—and came down on to the ground floor, into reality.

This move was absolutely necessary for them both. The divine side had been constellated. Raphael was already on his way, and such a phenomenon can only be faced from where we really belong, from our right place.

There was an immediate effect of this turning inward in Tobit. He realized that, as he had prayed for death, he must draw the consequences, prepare himself for death and give over the whole activity into the hands of his son Tobias. He had lost all the property they had, but in his extremity remembered money which he had left in trust with Gabael in Rages of Media and decided to send Tobias to fetch it.

As the book is quite well known, I will cut a long story short and only remind you that, after many admonitions, Tobit told Tobias to go to

Gabael and to seek a "trusty man" to accompany him. The archangel Raphael offered himself as Tobias's companion but without revealing his divine origin. In fact, when pressed by Tobit, he even invented a kinship with Tobit, as the son of Ananias the Great. Everything was thus in order and in spite of the lamentations of Anna, Tobit's wife, the two young men started their journey.

A charming touch here is that we are told that the young man's dog "went forth and journeyed with them." As far as I could gather from Cruden's Concordance, Tobias's dog is practically unique in either the Old Testament or its Apocrypha. If dogs are mentioned at all, it is negatively. But here the dog goes as companion and is mentioned in both the outward and homeward journeys. This would mean psychologically that Tobias—in contradistinction to his father, who lived by the law—was friendly with his instinct, and took it with him, which presumably had a very favorable effect on the success of his mission. After all, the Book of Tobit, in the form we now have it, was only written two or three centuries before the Oxyrhynchus Sayings of Jesus, where Jesus says it is the birds and fish that "draw us to the kingdom of heaven."[65] The new form of the "light of God" is evidently going to include a more instinctive approach. Moreover, only a man who is on good terms with his instinct has any chance of being up to an animus-possessed girl like Sarah.

On the first night of the journey—although Raphael had been sent by God to help Tobit and Sarah—it was the young man and not the angel who took the active role. It is not always so on these journeys of human and divine companions. Khidr, for instance, took all the action on his journey with Moses, as reported in the Koran, and in myths and fairy stories it is more usual for the companion with the divine or magical qualities to accomplish the heroic deeds. The divine is approaching nearer to the human being in our story, or, one could say, the human being is taking over more responsibility.

If we take the story from the masculine side, Tobias would represent *the archetypal foundation of all conscious egos,* as Dr. von Franz defines this archetype. But if, as now, we take it from the feminine side, Tobias would represent the archetypal basis—not of the ego—but of the transformed and integrated feminine mind.

---

[65] M.R. James, trans., *The Apocrypha of the New Testament,* p. 26.

The fact that Tobias took the action here corresponds to the alchemical idea that man must do the work himself, but it only succeeds *Deo concedente,* God willing. This divine consent is symbolized in our story by the presence of Raphael and the advice that he gives Tobias.

Time forbids me to enter into the rich symbolism of the fish, although it is important for our story. Fortunately Jung's *Aion* is now translated into English and you can find it there in considerable detail.[66] I will only just mention the aspect of the fish which is connected with the goddesses of Asia Minor. The Syrian goddess Atargatis, often called Derketo, is even described as the fish-goddess. Atargatis is related to the Greek Aphrodite; in fact the origin of this famous goddess is closely connected with the Babylonian love-goddesses and thus with the fish. We have already met with the birds of Aphrodite—the sparrows—blinding and thus depotentiating the tradition-bound Tobit. And now we see that this same goddess of love is also connected with the fish which represents the redeeming and healing substance of our story. One therefore suspects that the repressed eros, the feminine principle, which had no chance whatever in the narrow masculine dogma of Tobit or in the animus-possessed Sarah, is working behind the scenes to come into its own and to reestablish a balance between the two main opposites, masculine and feminine.

Here again our story is relevant to the present age. Two thousand years of a prevailing masculine religion have also greatly disturbed our psychic balance and—although the outer symptoms are totally different—it is sometimes possible to recognize the struggling eros principle trying to come into her own behind some of the catastrophic events of our time.

The opposites are completely split apart in our story, but this is more obvious in the dark and light principles than in the masculine and feminine, as is indeed also the case in our own day. Raphael represents the Mal'akh Jahwe on the light side, a creature of the spirit, an angel of grace, purely positive, whereas Asmodaeus is seen as purely negative, dark, evil and destructive, bound in the body, a chthonic creature of the *materia.* If Raphael had taken up the fight with Asmodaeus directly, it would have been a case of equal opposites and the result would have been quite uncertain. But by taking something material, the fish, from the realm of Asmodaeus, he had a far better chance, for, as we know, *similia similibus curan-*

---

[66] CW 9ii, pars. 162ff. [The Book of Tobit is mentioned in par. 174.—Ed.]

tur (like is cured by like).

Indeed, not the whole fish is required for the healing process, but an essence of it. The heart and the liver were selected by Raphael to drive out Asmodaeus, and the gall to cure Tobit's blindness. The liver could almost be described as life itself, and the heart is the mainspring of the body. Both are closely connected with the emotions and would therefore have the necessary intensity and warmth to drive away Sarah's inhuman incubus. But we must also ask why Raphael told Tobias that it was not the organs themselves but the smoke arising from burning them that would put the arch-demon to flight.

The idea of turning material things into smoke and steam always has to do with spiritualization, but here it has a more specific nuance. In his essay "On the Nature of the Psyche," Jung uses the simile of the ultraviolet and infrared ends of the spectrum, the latter representing instinct per se, and the former representing the spirit.[67] He points out that sinking into the instinctive (infrared) sphere only leads to unconsciousness and panic and not to a conscious realization and assimilation of the instinct. This can only take place at the spiritual (ultraviolet) end, where the archetype, as the image of the instinct, offers an opportunity to rescue consciousness from the boiling abyss of the passions and instincts.

This gives us some idea of why the heart and liver of the fish must be burned and thus spiritualized, for it is only at this end of the scale that consciousness can be renewed and strengthened. Sarah is enchanted by the old opinionated form of the animus, contaminated, even personified, by the collective arch-devil Asmodaeus. It will require a tremendous conscious realization before he can be made to give way in her and leave her free to receive the renewed and transformed animus, symbolized by Tobias.

After the adventure with the fish, the journey continued and, as they approached their first goal, the house of Raguel, Sarah's father, Raphael told Tobias about these unknown relations of his. He told him that he must marry Sarah and described her as a "wise, steadfast, and exceedingly honorable" maid. He also said that Raguel would be obliged to give her to Tobias because he was her nearest relation.

One is at first very surprised to hear a demon-possessed girl described in such glowing terms. But superlative qualities could almost be said to be

---

[67] *The Structure and Dynamics of the Psyche,* CW 8, pars. 414ff.

the *sine qua non* of being able to meet the dark in oneself. Jung pointed out recently that we have never been more in need of the Christian virtues than just now, when we are faced with a dark night of the soul and an unprecedented advance of the negative principle.

Very frequently in analysis—often when people learn to know their dark side for the first time—they tend to identify with their undesirable qualities and to lose sight of their virtues. This is very unwise, for the brighter their virtues, the darker their shadow, and one never cancels the other. So now, just as they are going to face the evil demon in Sarah, Raphael emphasizes her light side, so that Tobias may know she is a complete woman, with an unusually light side to balance the very dark Asmodaeus.

Though Tobias seemed to know very little of his kinsmen, he had heard of Sarah's demon and the fate of her seven husbands. He said simply: "Now for my part I fear." This is a very instinctive reaction, simple and direct, like the dog he brought with him, and one suspects his seven predecessors of having been very much lacking in instinct. The first, and even the second, may perhaps be excused but after that it was just folly not to be consciously fearful. Only a man with instinct can deal with an animus-possessed woman, and Tobias's fear here, like the fear of God, is proverbially the beginning of wisdom.

Raphael met this by reminding Tobias of his father's injunction to take a wife of his own kindred and—repeating his instructions regarding the burning of the fish's heart and liver to drive out Asmodaeus—told him that the demon would not hurt him, adding: "And fear not for she was set apart for thee before the world was, and thou shalt save her and she shall go with thee."

It is rather startling to meet here with such a clear reference to the later doctrine of predestination. Taken psychologically, and not pushed to extremes, this doctrine definitely has its part in the process of individuation. It is just as impossible to deviate from our own essential pattern as it would be for an apple to become a pear, or a tiger an innocent lamb. From this point of view, the liberated Sarah would be the anima in Tobias's pattern and Tobias the transformed animus in Sarah's. This would also explain the peculiar words with which this sixth chapter ends: "And when Tobias heard the words of Raphael and that she [Sarah] was his sister of the seed of his father's house, he loved her exceedingly and his heart clave unto her."

Tobias has not yet seen Sarah, so except on the assumption that she basically belongs to him as part of himself, as his anima, or that he is her animus or unconscious mind who needs just Sarah and no other to incarnate in this world, it would be difficult to explain how he could already love her. As it is, one is reminded of Goethe's famous words: "Were you not, in a former existence, my sister or my bride?"—which Jung often quoted as an example of how a man feels when he first meets his anima projected onto a real woman.

Raphael and Tobias then arrived at Raguel's house, where Tobias was immediately recognized by his likeness to Tobit. They were welcomed most hospitably, a ram was killed, and they were invited to sit down to supper. But Tobias refused to eat until his marriage with Sarah was arranged. Raguel consented and made a clean breast of the past. Evidently he was certain that Tobias would meet the same fate as the other husbands, and even dug the young man's grave secretly in the night.

Raguel, like old Tobit, reveals himself here as a burier of the dead, bound to the pessimistic certainty that everything will go on in the same old negative way, a tendency we still see frequently in a woman's animus, especially if there is a strong father complex. Raguel apparently believed implicitly in the power of Asmodaeus. In fact one wonders if there were not a secret bond between them, for Sarah was his only child and fathers often have great difficulty in parting with their daughters. Asmodaeus himself reminds one vividly of the animus in his role as jealous lover or husband, for he never harmed Sarah but just killed his rivals.

Tobias was not infected by Raguel's pessimism and went on refusing to eat until Sarah was given to him "according to the law of Moses." He showed great wisdom here, for though he was the renewer of consciousness, he did not throw the old and traditional reality away but insisted on using it to legitimize his new position.

From Sarah's point of view, we must here consider the different aspects of her animus. Up until now her father had been her only human love. She showed real feeling for him when, even in her despair, she resisted hanging herself for his sake. Behind her father, however, was the archetypal figure of the arch-demon. But when she prayed to God in her extremity, He sent Raphael who, it is true, only entered her consciousness now, but who undoubtedly had his effect before in holding Asmodaeus in check, for there are no more murders after her prayer. These three are now joined by the pivotal fourth: Tobias. He would represent a transformed mind in Sarah, hitherto entirely unconscious, but a mind that began to develop and become active when she decided to live on and endure the suffering caused by Asmodaeus. She was now obliged to risk everything, for if the demon succeeded in killing Tobias she was lost indeed.

When the document was signed, they sat down to eat the ram. The symbolism of the ram is very interesting here, for as the spring sign it represents the virility and masculine strength which first had to be sacrificed and then integrated (eaten) by Tobias, before he was ready for the acid test: the encounter with Asmodaeus.

After supper the bridal pair were led to their chamber. Tobias exactly carried out the instructions of Raphael, and Asmodaeus escaped from the smoke to "the upper parts of Egypt," where Raphael bound him again. The fact that he was bound at the sources of the Nile indicates that he was once again repressed and banished to the depths of the unconscious, a procedure which was absolutely necessary at that time. Even a few centuries later, in the Book of Revelation, you will remember that Satan was bound for a thousand years. This binding of the animus is still sometimes necessary in certain cases, such as when there is contamination by an collective demon or by a psychotic streak, but we have no time to go into that here.

It is interesting that Raphael—who could be regarded psychologically as the equal opposite of Asmodaeus—was now able to overcome and bind him. Presumably this could be achieved because of the steadfast attitude of the human beings who not only used the symbol of the love goddess as instructed, but accepted her completely in opening their hearts to love. This creative attitude strengthened the positive side and enabled it to banish destruction, at least for a time.

When the baffled demon had fled, Tobias and Sarah shut the door of their room and—again following the instructions of Raphael—prayed together before they embraced. This prayer was absolutely necessary, for the victory was brought about by the direct intervention of God and, if they had taken the credit to themselves, the consequent inflation would have brought back old Asmodaeus, the opinionated demon, as strong as ever.

Tobias especially says: "I take not this my sister for lust but in truth." It is at the ultraviolet, spiritual end of the scale—"in truth"—that the realization, the new consciousness, must be born. Only a great effort to reach this end, symbolized here by their joint prayer to God, will suffice to find the truth which alone can prevent this new consciousness from being swallowed again by the dark, emotional, instinctive unconscious.

Raguel and his wife Edna were overjoyed (at any rate consciously) to find Tobias alive and well in the morning. Raguel organized a prolonged and rich wedding feast, designed to keep the young people with him as long as possible. But Tobias was eager to get home, to present his bride to old Tobit and to cure his blindness. Raphael helped him by collecting the debt from Gabael, and (resisting the eager entreaties of Raguel) Raphael, Tobias, Sarah and the dog all traveled back to Tobit with half of Raguel's great possessions as Sarah's dowry, as well as the money from Gabael. At the angel's suggestion, Tobias and Raphael went ahead and the fish was put to its second use: Tobit's sight was restored.

Presumably Tobias had to attend to the kindling of the new light of consciousness first, symbolized by the healing of Sarah and the new *coniunctio*. Only when this light was burning brightly, firmly established as it were, could it be seen even by the eyes of the old traditional Tobit, as God intended, for Raphael was sent to earth not only to cure Sarah but also that Tobit might see "the light of God," the new consciousness. Tobit himself connected this light with his son, and what his son had achieved. This is clear in his first exclamation when the scales had fallen from his eyes: "I see thee, child, the light of mine eyes."

Tobit, once more a well-to-do man, also gave a wedding feast in honor of the marriage. They considered all that Raphael had done for them and decided to reward him with half of everything brought home. Then, and only then, did Raphael reveal to them that he was no ordinary kinsman but an archangel sent by God. He was apparently surprised himself that they had never noticed that he had neither eaten nor drunk, and he repeated more than once that he was "a vision which appeared to you."

Even now we hear that they were "troubled," "fell upon their faces" and "were afraid." So we see why the fact of Raphael's divine origin had not dawned on them before. Everything had to be put in order, and the new consciousness stabilized by the marriage and Tobit's restored sight, before they would be able to stand the shock. Had Tobias, in the course of the journey, recovered from his fear, still the knowledge that he was traveling with an archangel could have tempted him to behave like a child, blindly relying on his divine companion. He would have had far less chance to grow up, to take the initiative himself, even sometimes to defend the point of view of consciousness against the unconscious, by such naive remarks as: "For my part I fear." Moreover it is characteristic of the most difficult situations—such as this journey depicts—that the divine plan is only seen later; we must suffer it more or less blindly at the time.

Up until this point, although marvelous things had happened, it all seemed entirely within the frame of the normal. Tobit was impoverished, but this was put right by the debt being repaid and the appearance of a rich daughter-in-law. Sarah had been rid of her demon, but that could be regarded as the direct result of the burning of the fish's heart and liver: a medical therapy; which also applies to the gall of the fish removing the scales from Tobit's eyes. But these happy events had been piling up, until they were all now ready for the real revelation, namely the numinous fact that this was all divine handiwork and that they had seen the messenger of God who now revealed the hidden and numinous pattern in which they all had their part.

Psychologically this would mean that only at the end were any of them ready for this most difficult realization of all in the process of individuation: the realization of the divine, utterly unknown, part of man. Jung has even said that recognizing the shadow, and all the things pertaining to the ego which we have repressed, is the merest child's play compared to the effort that is required to penetrate this unknown realm. This hidden divine part of man is beautifully symbolized in our story by the intimate daily contact with the unrecognized archangel.

We must now consider whether our story has revealed anything that is of practical use to us in understanding the religious function of the animus in woman today. But we should first establish what we mean by the term "religious function." I use it really in contradistinction to the old opinionated animus which is the original condition in practically every woman. As you know, just as men suffer from anima moods, so women suffer from a whole network of animus opinions that consist very largely of what the father, or other male authorities of their youth, taught them, or what they gathered unconsciously of their *Weltanschauung.* Such opinions have an absolute and exceedingly emotional character. We do not question them, they are too ingrained. The woman simply believes and asserts them as indisputable facts.

The religious function of the animus really begins when the woman has the courage to doubt the absolute truth of her opinions. This is far more difficult than it sounds, for animus certainty is a tremendous support on which many women lean unconsciously, exactly as the traditional wife could lean on her husband. Moreover, the animus can impart a deceptive but very seductive feeling of being always right. Certainty is always one-sided, and directly we allow the opposite to live we become prey to doubt. But at the same time, in place of the certainty the animus lent us before, we have a dim feeling that in all this doubt, suffering and uncertainty, there is somewhere a purpose, perhaps even a divine purpose, that it is not all in vain.

Jung once said in a seminar that man overcomes by killing the dragon, by masculine activity, whereas woman can only overcome in a more passive way, by accepting her suffering. If she can accept the suffering involved in changing her old certainty for doubt, the animus himself begins to change. He no longer supplies her with false and off-the-mark opinions, but begins himself to search in the doubt and darkness for hints, for small indications, that show the way to the divine pattern of the process of individuation. Instead of possessing and tyrannizing the ego, he begins himself to serve the Self, to become a religious function which can help the ego in its lifelong task of discovering the Self, the divine part of us.

We will now return to our story and see how it bears out these few theoretical remarks on the religious function of the animus.

The state described at the beginning, if somewhat extreme and dramatic, is very much the state of the animus in almost any woman before she begins the task of working on it. The two father figures, Tobit and Raguel, are both caught in tradition and the past. Tobit is entirely preoccupied with the dead and Raguel is firmly convinced that nothing can change but must go on in the old negative, destructive way. With such a foundation for her animus opinions, Sarah was wide open to possession. As an arch-demon, Asmodaeus was admittedly a more potent and destructive figure that, fortunately, usually preoccupies himself with an ordinary woman. But the difference is only in degree; a demon possession of a more modest kind is practically always the result of such a paternal background.

The turning point comes when Sarah—after the reproaches of the maid-servant, which show her how the ordinary, instinctive woman regards her—decides against giving up the battle by hanging herself, and decides to accept her almost intolerable suffering. She herself makes the first turn toward the religious attitude, in her prayer to God. If He will not let her die, then He must hear her reproach. Such a desperate appeal—accompanied with the real sacrifice of going on with her life—is seldom unheard and the divine side of the psyche comes into action. In psychological language, the ego sacrifices itself and asks the Self to take over.

The Self does so very efficiently: it sends Raphael to help. This divine element is unrecognized until the end of the story, as is usually the case with us. But it is not only the archetypal background that reacts. Simultaneously, Tobit gives over the action to his son, Tobias, who, as a human being, can be regarded as Sarah's individual animus.

Tobias did indeed take over the religious function of the animus. Directly his father entrusted him with the task of collecting the money from Gabael—that is, a sum of energy lying untouched and unused in the unconscious—he began to look for hints to lead him on the way to fulfill the pattern. It was he who found Raphael and brought him to his father and, right through their journey, he allowed himself to be guided by the suggestions dropped by the Archangel, even where he had to overcome a most justifiable fear.

A great deal of this happened in the unconscious for Sarah, as indeed it often does for the woman of today. If she can once make up her mind to a completely new attitude toward life and her animus, the latter often changes without her knowledge. I have seen more than one case where the woman was as agreeably surprised as Sarah, when her Tobias broke through into consciousness.

Sarah accepted Tobias immediately and from then on, seen from the point of view of her psychology, the action was conscious. Together they carried out Raphael's suggestions and thus reached a *coniunctio* "in truth," which symbolizes the "light of God"—in psychological language, a new consciousness.

In conclusion, we should perhaps consider the images of the Self in this story from the standpoint of Sarah's psychology. As you know, the images of the Self in dreams tend to be of the same sex as the dreamer, although this is by no means an invariable rule. There are certain indications of a feminine divine figure, working behind the scenes, in the sparrows of Aphrodite and the fish goddesses of Asia Minor. But these are mere hints, hidden behind the one great overwhelming figure of Raphael. Angels have a certain sexless quality and at bottom the Self, as a union of opposites, is hermaphroditic. Therefore I suggest that Raphael (not forgetting his shadow Asmodaeus) is the image of the Self in our story, whether you take it from the masculine or feminine side.

We must not, however, forget that Tobit's and Sarah's prayers were "heard before the glory of God" and that in response He sent His archangel to help them both. Then we hear no more of Him; everything is done by Raphael. Looked at psychologically, this exactly corresponds to the archetype per se which, as Jung has said in so many places, is entirely beyond our apprehension. It is only in its images that we can apprehend and experience it, just as in our story it was Raphael who was experienced so intimately by all the characters, but especially by Tobias.

Therefore, Tobias seems to me to represent equally well the archetypal basis of man's ego consciousness that must actively overcome the dragon (Asmodaeus), and as the religious function of the animus in woman that will help her actively if she accepts her suffering and learns the value of her own feminine principle. Tobias above all represents the spirit of ultimate, genuine integrity.

6
The Problem of Contact with Animus

(February 16, 1951)

One often hears the complaint, even from people who have been studying Jungian psychology for years, that too much is said about the theory and too little about how this theory works out in everyday life. This point of view seems to me particularly constellated at present, for it has never been more obvious that invisible forces are at work which human reason is totally unable to control. The only place where there is any hope of our being able to come to terms with these forces, as Jung has pointed out again and again, is in the individual. Therefore it seems particularly necessary to devote this paper as much as possible to the strictly practical side. But any reader who has made such an attempt knows the enormous difficulties which such a venture involves. We can only touch on a fragment of the vast tangle of problems with which our theme confronts us.

By the term animus I understand the masculine spirit or unconscious mind of woman. Emma Jung pointed out recently that one should differentiate very carefully here between the anima and the animus. The anima, as is well known, is Jung's term for the feminine soul of man. But it is really a contradiction in terms to speak of the animus—as was done in the early days of Jungian psychology and often still today—as the masculine soul of woman. The word animus means "spirit" and the contrast between soul (anima) and spirit (animus) gives us a valuable hint as to the difference between the two figures.

One might say that when a man takes up the problem of his anima, he is attempting to find the "inherited, collective image of woman" which exists in his own unconscious, with the help of which he is able to comprehend the nature of woman, as Jung expresses it.[68] At the same time he finds his own unconscious function of relationship. Therefore in his search for the anima, the goal of man is at bottom to find the function of relationship which he has always projected onto woman. The goal of woman,

---

[68] "Anima and Animus," *Two Essays on Analytical Psychology,* CW 7, par. 301.

on the other hand, is to find the inherited collective image of the spirit or mind which she has always projected onto man. The mind of woman— inasmuch as it is unconscious— is autonomous and projected to an almost incredible extent although she is usually unaware of this fact.

The problem of modern woman in this respect is most clearly described in Jung's essay, "Woman in Europe," with all the symptoms which surround us on every side proving that the masculine side of woman can no longer be denied. Jung says there:

> Masculinity means knowing what one wants and doing what is necessary to achieve it. Once this has been learned it is so obvious that it can never again be forgotten without tremendous psychic loss.[69]

If we are to avoid this "tremendous psychic loss," therefore, we are obliged sooner or later to face the problem of the animus.

The spotlight in this paper is definitely on the animus and not on the anima, for it is only of the former that I can speak from direct personal experience, which is the only firm ground when one comes to the practical side. Nevertheless, a good deal of what is said also applies to the anima, particularly as regards the technique for coming to terms with these figures. The passages quoted above, for instance, are taken from a place where Jung is speaking primarily of the anima. The main difference that one must always keep in mind is that, where a woman reacts with rigid opinions which go irritatingly beside the mark, a man is inclined to react with moods or with a peculiarly touchy vanity. In other words, a woman's unconscious reactions are inclined to be those of a somewhat inferior man and vice versa.

All the Jungian psychology in this paper naturally comes from Jung, begged, borrowed or stolen! What I am attempting to do—for undoubtedly the reader has read the psychology infinitely better in Jung's own books— is to give a modest report of how it seems to me that Jung's ideas work out when women attempt to apply them in their own psychology. Of course, when a woman writes of the animus, she is always up against the fact that the animus himself may have his own views on the matter. Jung once pointed out in a seminar that whereas portraits of the anima are exceedingly common in literature, good portraits of the animus are rare. He thought this must be because the animus himself to a great extent writes

---

[69] *Civilization in Transition,* CW 10, par. 260.

the books of women and prefers not to give himself away. (The anima, on the other hand, seems to be rather fond of sitting for her portrait!) Therefore I never feel quite sure how much the animus, like a wily old fox, is obliterating his track with his brush.

The Predominance of the Unconscious in the Personality

The first point on which we must agree before entering on our theme is the fact that the psyche reaches far beyond our conscious knowledge. The idea that we are really the master in our own house and the pernicious slogan, "Where there's a will, there's a way," both die hard. I emphasize this because, long after we have realized the existence of both personal and collective unconscious, and are quite aware that we have a shadow and an animus or anima, we find ourselves behaving exactly as if we did not know it at all. It is not easy to shake off the nineteenth-century rational ideas with which we and our immediate forefathers grew up and which still flourish around us.

When we realize that the psyche itself extends far beyond our ego and its conscious knowledge, we are confronted with the fact that we live in an unknown, invisible country. There is indeed a great deal of comparative material from which we can gather information. Primitives, for instance, have at most one leg in outside reality and the other in this invisible world. What they call the land of the spirits is to them the greater reality of the two, and studying their ways of dealing with their spirits can be compared to reading a description of the country before taking a journey. We can also find comparative material in many other fields. I mention, for instance, the great religions, both of East and West, the Gnostic systems, alchemy and, on a lower level, witchcraft and magic.

We may say, however, that all secondhand accounts of what Jung calls the collective unconscious have only a relative value. They are absolutely invaluable in amplification and comparison, but the *sine qua non* of any real knowledge of the unconscious is actual experience. It cannot be emphasized too often that psychology is an empirical science. Jungian psychology especially is frequently misunderstood as a philosophy or even a religion, but always by people who have had no experience of it themselves and who therefore find reports of other people's actual experience so strange that they assume it must be a matter of philosophical or mystical speculation. They are really more or less in the position of people listening to an explorer's account of some strange tribe whose habits are so different to their own that the listener may involuntarily find himself thinking: "He is pulling the long bow," or "fishermen's tales." Some people go even further and, when something from the unconscious catches them and forces them to experience it, they think they are seeing "white mice" or say, like the man when he first saw a duck-billed platypus: "Why, there ain't no such bird."

Yet, we have not very far to seek for evidence that we are moved by things within ourselves which differ from our conscious personality. How often do we say: "What possessed me to do that?" Or we are angry with ourselves because we have done the exact opposite from what we intended. Yet, somehow, we hate to draw the logical conclusion, and even doubt the evidence of our own senses, rather than face the alarming fact that there are forces within us that act independently and oblige us to carry out their intentions. They are what we call complexes.

The following incident may illustrate the difficulty of admitting unusual facts. A storm on the Lake of Zurich once detached a floating public bathing establishment from its moorings at the upper end of the lake. It was on a winter's night and it drifted right down the lake to near Zurich before it was discovered and towed back to its base. This peculiar incident was related at a dinner party that night and a young woman exclaimed with relief: "I saw a bathing establishment in the middle of the lake from my window this morning, but of course I did not mention it because I knew it really could not be there!" She was unable to admit the evidence of her own eyes until she was provided with a rational explanation, and we constantly miss the most obvious psychic facts due to the same prejudice.

Jung, in his seminar on Nietzsche's *Thus Spake Zarathustra,* spoke of the realization that we consist not only of consciousness but also of the unconscious, and that our conscious will is constantly being crossed by unconscious wills in ourselves. He said:

> It is as if you were ruler of a land which is only partially known to yourself, king of a country with an unknown number of inhabitants. You do not know who they are or what their condition may be: time and again you make the discovery that you have subjects in your country of whose existence you had no idea. Therefore you cannot assume the responsibility, you can only say: "I find myself as the ruler of a country which has unknown borders and unknown inhabitants, with qualities of which I am not entirely aware." Then you are at once out of your subjectivity, and are

confronted with a situation in which you are a sort of prisoner: you are confronted with unknown possibilities, because those many uncontrollable factors at any time may influence all your actions or decisions. So you are a funny kind of king in that country, a king who is not really a king, who is dependent upon so many unknown quantities and conditions that he often cannot carry through his own intentions. Therefore it is better not to speak of being a king at all, and be only one of the inhabitants who has just a corner of that territory in which to rule. And the greater your experience, the more you see that your corner is infinitely small in comparison with the vast extent of the unknown against you.[70]

Once we have realized that we are not the king in our psyche, not the master in our own house, we are—paradoxically enough—in a much stronger position. We have escaped from our subjectivity, that is, we have gained a tiny piece of objective ground where we can stand and look around us. A great deal that belongs in our own inner world has always been in projection: those things which we do not see in ourselves are automatically projected into our environment. We do not make projections but we find pieces of ourselves—parts we have not recognized—projected into our environment. How many of us have a favorite *bête noir,* for instance, who conveniently carries all the qualities that we do not want to recognize as our own? It is nearly seven hundred years since **Meister Eckhart** exclaimed: "It is all inside, not outside, for everything is inside." But how few people have realized as yet what he meant.

The Shadow

When we experience the fact that our conscious ego is only an inhabitant in a small corner of a vast territory, we naturally want to know something about the other inhabitants. Before Jung, the unconscious—insofar as it had been recognized at all—was mainly regarded as repressed material which could just as well be conscious. The latter is quite true—at any rate in theory—of what Jung calls the personal unconscious. The shadow—in its personal aspects—has its home in this layer. In some passages Jung even identifies the two, and it could therefore be called our nearest neighbor in the vast extent of the unknown which surrounds us. It is clear that considerable knowledge of the shadow is required before we are in a position to take up our problem with the more distant figures, including the animus.

The shadow is a minor figure in oneself which is the exact negative of

---

[70] *Nietzsche's* Zarathustra, vol. 1, p. 390.

the conscious personality. One usually regards it as something inferior and, in its commonest form, it is composed of all the negative qualities which one does not want to see in oneself. But, in the case of people who are living below their possibilities, the shadow can contain very positive qualities, as Jung often pointed out.

In its personal aspect, the shadow is not really difficult to recognize, although this is a long, weary and often exceedingly painful undertaking. The real difficulty comes from the contamination of the personal shadow with figures of the collective unconscious behind it. This represents a great complication of the work. For instance, people with a sensitive conscience, once they see their dark side at all, may lose their sense of proportion and begin to make themselves responsible for the devil himself! Therefore, learning to discriminate between the personal sphere and the great figures of the collective unconscious is of the utmost importance.

The figure nearest to the ego and shadow is the anima or animus. Jung often speaks of a kind of marriage between the animus and the shadow, which makes a combination that is far too strong for the weak conscious ego. In a 1932 Seminar, he goes into this aspect in considerable detail and points out that a woman must be in possession of her shadow—that is, aware of her inferior side—in order to be in a position to relate to her animus at all. People who think they are just too marvelously good and thus deny their shadows altogether are, he says, literally *"possessed* by devils":

> They are all eaten up by the animus and the animus grows fat on it, he is strengthened by that excellent nourishment, he gets so strong that he can possess the conscious and then the conscious is under his rule. Therefore the animus should not be connected with the shadow, that connection should be broken, despite the fact that you arrive at the animus by way of the shadow; for you can never arrive at the animus unless you see the shadow, unless you see your own inferior sides. When you see your shadow, you can detach from the anima or animus, but as long as you don't see it you have not got a ghost of a chance.[71]

To put it still more simply: You haven't a ghost of a chance while the animus and shadow are married, for the game always stands at two to one against the conscious ego. We shall see further on what it means psychologically to be "possessed by devils," and we shall also return later to the role of the shadow in our problem of contact with the animus.

---

[71] *The Visions Seminars,* p. 211 (modified).

Making the Acquaintance of the Animus

It is a well-known fact, quite outside psychological circles, that the soul (anima) of man frequently presents herself in personified, feminine form. I mention only Dante's "Beatrice," Petrarch's "Laura," and Rider Haggard's "She." But the fact that the spirit of woman presents itself in masculine form seems to me much less well known. Had anyone drawn this conclusion at all clearly until Jung recognized this counterpart to the anima in the unconscious of women? Now that we have realized the empirical existence of this figure, this spontaneous product of the unconscious, we can find traces of it in many places, though often in a negative form. The demons that possessed women, for instance, were usually of the masculine sex. I mention, for instance, Asmodaeus, the evil spirit in the Book of Tobit who possessed Sarah and killed her seven husbands, before Tobit, with the help of the angel Raphael, exorcised the devil by means of the heart and liver of a fish. Moreover, the "little master" of the witches and the "Grand Master" of the covens were almost always masculine.

The fact that the Christian God, particularly the Protestant God, is exclusively masculine presumably made it more difficult for woman than for man to recognize her individual spirit, for it was always projected. This may be one of many reasons why woman realized the existence of her male counterpart so many centuries later than man. I mention this only in passing, for it would lead us too far from our subject to continue this theme.

It should be mentioned that in earlier and more peaceful days, when the unconscious fitted smoothly into the prevailing religion, the great majority of people could find the answer to all these questions—if indeed they were even asked—within the tenets of their faith. There are indeed fortunate people today whose unconscious still fits in the framework of some established religion, and such people should on no account be disturbed, for, in these chaotic days, a real hold of any kind in the invisible world is of the greatest value, not only to themselves but also to their surroundings.

I experienced this vividly last autumn when I went to a Catholic village in Switzerland for a weekend. It contains an unusual amount of rest homes for Catholics, largely for monks and nuns. I immediately experienced a feeling of the most extraordinary peace in the village, which I at first attributed to the herds of cows, the mountains, the turning leaves and the mellow autumnal sun. But, shortly before, I had spent my holiday in a place where all these things were present, without experiencing anything of this unusual feeling of inner security. The friend I was with has considerable resistances to the Church and was always mildly grumbling at the amount of priests and nuns whom we met. I was therefore astonished to hear her say suddenly: "I know why it is so peaceful: their religion is really holding the unconscious of these people. They are not split underneath as we are."

But desirable as that condition may be, today it is rather the exception than the rule. Particularly the people who come to psychology are usually suffering from some kind of disharmony within themselves. It is true that in the majority of cases this disharmony is projected onto the outer world, so the conscious problem is that in one way or another they are at odds with their environment.

I remember Dr. Jung saying some fifteen years ago, when he was still in the thick of his practice, that almost everyone came to him for a different reason. In the majority of cases, it sufficed to give help with the outer difficulties, to open up a new attitude toward them, for instance, or to point out things that had been overlooked. As he also emphasizes in his writings, it is only a small minority that is destined to tread the difficult inner way of coming to terms with the collective unconscious, that "longest of all paths," as the alchemists call it. It is this minority whom I have in mind when I speak of the problem of contact with the animus.

Once we have definitely realized that we have a shadow and are no longer naively projecting all our own bad qualities onto our unfortunate neighbors, and are also aware that our consciousness is only an infinitely small corner in comparison with the vast extent of the unknown within us, we have gained a piece of firm ground from which we can begin the task of making the acquaintance of our anima or animus. On the one hand these figures have a personal aspect so that we can talk of *my* animus or *my* anima, but, on the other, they are also inhabitants of the collective unconscious, so that it sometimes seems far more correct, as Jung noted, to speak of *the* animus and *the* anima.[72] In quarrels between two women, for instance, the matter often becomes hopelessly confused if they make an attempt to find out who was to blame. And when they first study psychology and begin informing each other that they are quite willing to grant it was the *other's* animus, the matter usually goes from bad to worse! But in

---

[72] "The Psychology of the Transference," *The Practice of Psychotherapy,* CW 16, par. 469.

time, when they can see that the whole quarrel was arranged by *the* animus and that both were more or less his victims, they can often gain a piece of objective ground from which a real understanding can be reached.

In the spring of 1938, toward the end of his seminar on *Zarathustra*, Jung went into this matter in some detail. He was speaking of the projection of the dark side and of seeing the devil projected into someone else. He pointed out that, in analysis, the patient is gradually convinced that he "cannot assume Mr. So-and-So to be the arch-devil" who can interfere seriously with his soul. But the first result of seeing this projection is often introjection: the patient assumes that he himself is the devil. Nothing is gained by this, for of course the patient is not the devil either, so the latter "falls back into the sauce and dissolves there." Then the analyst has to say: "Now look here, in spite of the fact that you say there is no terrible devil, there is at least a psychological fact that you might *call* the devil." Then the analyst might go on to suggest constructing a devil so as to provide a form or vessel in which the returning projection can be caught.[73]

There has been a general belief, in almost every form of human society, in some kind of personification of evil per se. And it is inevitable that we shall either project collective forces onto our neighbors, or introject them into ourselves, if we do not allow for the reality of the figures of the collective unconscious. Therefore it seems to me of vital importance that we should never forget that the animus—however personally we may take him—is *also* a figure of the collective unconscious.

In another seminar, Jung pointed out that as soon as a woman begins controlling her animus, or a man his anima, they come up against the herd instinct in mankind. Man's original state was one of complete unconsciousness and this condition still persists in us all today. As soon as we attempt to liberate ourselves from possession by the anima or animus, we arrive at a different order of things, which means a challenge to the old order. If one sheep goes by itself ahead of the flock, it will seem like a

---

[73] *Nietzsche's* Zarathustra: *Notes of the Seminar Given in 1934-1939*, vol. 2, pp. 1320f. It should not be overlooked that Jung was speaking of Nietsche's Zarathustra and pointing out that, as Nietzsche had constructed the figure of Zarathustra, the light aspect of the Self, he should have constructed a counter-shadow figure or the latter would, as indeed it did, fall into the "sauce" of his own psyche. Naturally there is always a certain danger in quoting passages out of context.

wolf to the others and thus be exposed to attack. Moreover, no sooner do you get rid of one devil than you have all the other devils against you:

> If a man makes a modest attempt at controlling his anima, he will be right away in a situation where he is tested to the blood; all the devils of the world will try to get into his anima in order to bring him back into the fold of mother nature. . . . The same with a woman: every devil circulating within 100 miles will do his best to get the goat of her animus.[74]

The truth of these words will be evident, I think, to any woman who has made a serious attempt to come to terms with her animus. The people in her environment are, on the one hand, fascinated by the fact that she has gained a standpoint *au-dessus de la mêlée* but, on the other, their unconscious—particularly their animus—is irritated by the fact that something has been done *contra naturam*. Therefore she often finds herself exposed to the most unexpected attacks, usually of a very irrational kind.

When we first face the fact, however, that we are only conscious of a small corner of our psyche, and that we have to reckon with another will or other wills in ourselves, we usually feel up against a multitude, a confusion that is hopelessly bewildering. The greatest help in this confusion usually comes from dreams. Here it is of the greatest value to turn to the experience of other people in order to learn what is already known about this dark, unknown realm in which our consciousness is set like a small island of light.

It is obvious that the animus—as a figure with both individual and collective characteristics—is particularly suitable to be a liaison officer, so to speak, between conscious and unconscious. It is true that as we first learn to know him, he seems to have little inclination for such a helpful role. This depends quite a lot on individual conditions: a woman with a positive relation to her father, for instance, has a certain subjective readiness—an innate psychic structure—for a positive experience with the male sex and with the animus. But this is often compensated in later life with a peculiarly devilish animus whose existence she has overlooked, and vice versa. The thing we must never forget in dealing with the animus is that he is dual; he always has a negative and positive aspect. (A fact which, of course, also applies to the anima.)

A woman I met years ago had a most helpful animus figure whom she

---

[74] *[The Visions Seminars,* pp. 243f. (modified).—Ed.]

called Archibald. She never did anything without consulting Archibald and, at first, she certainly seemed in a most enviable position. He always knew the right way out of the most desperate situations and, when I once heard a long account of his exploits, I own I was very much impressed. All the same, one could not help feeling even then that she was becoming too dependent on this figure, and one or two of us tried to warn her that it would be just as well to put a question mark against the omnipotence of Archibald. He had, however, already gained far more influence on her than could be balanced by any human voice, and she went on trusting herself wholeheartedly to his guidance.

It ended, as one might expect, in her becoming more and more possessed by this figure whose previous positive effect became progressively more negative. Had she been able to keep a critical standpoint of her own from which she could have recognized the dual nature of this figure, she would not have fallen into this trap.

It may seem strange to the reader that any sane woman could personify her unconscious mind or spirit to such an extent that she could consult him about her daily life and allude to him as Archibald. As we shall see later, it is indeed open to question whether she was wise to involve him so much in her outer life. But, as Jung points out so clearly, they do make themselves felt in such a way that one can best apprehend their reality by treating them as autonomous personalities with a life and will of their own. He says that taking them in a very personal way helps us to recognize their personality and makes it possible for us to establish a relationship with them.[75]

The experience of other people, as mentioned before, is usually insufficient to convince us right away that we really have a personified unconscious mind or spirit that is influencing us without our knowledge. Therefore we should briefly consider how we can catch the animus at work in ourselves and thus experience him first hand.

Perhaps the most usual and least unpleasant way of learning to know our animus is through our dreams, where he usually appears personified. It is there that we first learn to regard him as a person. The many forms he can take are well known, both negative and positive, human and demonic, animal and divine. He often appears as an authoritative figure, a priest or

---

[75] *Two Essays on Jungian Psychology,* CW 7, pars. 321ff.

monk, a teacher or ruler. He is particularly fond of telling us what we *should* do and of replacing our instincts with a network of opinions. He often appears in dreams as actual men we know or knew, as the father—the first carrier of his image—or as brother, husband, lover and so on.

The animus can also appear as a plurality. Jung mentioned *Christina Alberta's Father* by H.G. Wells more than once in his seminars as an example of the way the animus works in woman.[76] The girl does all sorts of nonsensical things during the day but in the evening she holds a sort of "court of conscience" which tells her exactly what she has really been up to. This is a kind of inexorable thinking which she cannot get away from and is a good illustration of the autonomous working of the unconscious mind of woman. The parrot Old Nick, in *Green Dolphin Country* by Elizabeth Goudge, plays a similar role. He is forever destroying Marianne's fictions about herself and always reappears with some crushing remark, just as she hopes he has succumbed in earthquake, war or fire.

One of the techniques Jung recommends for getting acquainted with our animus is to keep a sharp lookout on our speech and constantly to question our thoughts as they pass through our minds: Did *I* think that? Where did it come from? *Who* thought it? This is a most disagreeable technique and we always find good excuses to avoid it, such as never having time and so on. But if we can force ourselves to practice it, and to write down the outcome—for we forget such thoughts almost before we think them—the results are exceedingly instructive.

The place where the animus usually makes us most unhappy is when he interferes in our relationships. As mentioned before, the leading principle of women and the anima is eros, and that of men and the animus is logos. Whereas eros wishes to join and unite, the logos wishes to discriminate and for that purpose to separate. The animus, therefore, can have an exceedingly severing effect. If the relationship—to the husband, analyst or someone else—is important enough to us, we shall suffer a great deal in this respect. But this also forms an invaluable incentive to investigate and discover the animus. In fact, it is often just here that we become convinced of the reality of this figure which before we only accepted theoretically. When the opinions we have always taken for gospel separate us from someone who is vital to our feeling life, we may, for the first time, be

---

[76] E.g., ibid., par. 332.

willing to question their validity, where no logic or argument would have any effect whatsoever.[77]

It is also in our vital relationships to someone of the opposite sex that we usually first discover the animus in projection. As long as the projection fits, indeed, we are naturally unaware that it exists. But sooner or later, if the relationship is important enough, it is certain to give rise to trouble. This aspect of our problem is described in an unsurpassable way by Emma Jung in her excellent article, "A Contribution to the Problem of the Animus."[78]

Although there are exceptions, most women, when they have experienced the reality of the animus beyond all doubt, feel exceedingly negatively toward him. He is forever thwarting our intentions, spoiling our relationships, replacing our sound instincts and feelings by a mere collection of opinions, and altogether preventing us from living our lives naturally as women. This is only too true of the animus in his negative aspect, and when we experience only this side we are obliged sooner or later to ask ourselves: Why do I know so little of my own mind? Why am I on such bad terms with my animus? What am I doing that he always thwarts me? Obviously, early experiences with the projected animus—a negative father complex, for instance—play a great role here and must always be taken into account.[79] But as Jung says in *Psychology and Alchemy:*

> No matter how much parents and grandparents may have sinned against the child, the man who is really adult will accept these sins as his own condition which has to be reckoned with. Only a fool is interested in other people's guilt, since he cannot alter it. The wise man learns only from his own guilt. He will ask himself: Who am I that all this should happen to me? To find the answer to this fateful question he will look into his own heart.[80]

If then we decide to grow up, to become adult in the sense which Jung means here, and want to put the "fateful question" for which we must look

---

[77] There is a good deal about this in "The Psychology of the Transference," *The Practice of Psychotherapy,* CW 16, and also in chapter 3 of *Aion,* CW 9ii.

[78] [Later published as the first essay in Emma Jung's *Animus and Anima.*—Ed.]

[79] I do not emphasize the father complex in this paper because its effects are comparatively well known but, as these are exceedingly far-reaching, it would be a great mistake to underestimate them.

[80] CW 12, par. 152.

into our "own heart," we shall not be in a position to answer until we have had it out, or come to terms, with our own animus. Recall that the animus has a negative and a positive aspect. If we constantly run up against the negative side, we may assume—as is usually also the case in our human relationships—that we are failing to see his point of view.

Negotiations with the Animus

This brings us to a way of coming to terms with the animus, which is similar to the method Jung recommends to men for coming to terms with their inner woman:

> [A man] is quite right to treat the anima as an autonomous personality and to address personal questions to her.
>   . . . The art of it consists only in allowing our invisible partner to make herself heard, in putting the mechanism of expression momentarily at her disposal, without being overcome by the distaste one naturally feels at playing such an apparently ludicrous game with oneself, or by doubts as to the genuineness of the voice of one's interlocutor.[81]

> The technique of coming to terms with the animus is the same in principle as in the case of the anima; only here the woman must learn to criticize and hold her opinions at a distance; not in order to repress them, but, by investigating their origins, to penetrate more deeply into the background, where she will then discover the primordial images, just as the man does in his dealings with the anima.[82]

These conversations with anima or animus are a form of active imagination, a technique unsurpassed in providing a middle territory where conscious and unconscious can unite. It is, however, not a technique for everybody and is one that should not be used lightly for it has effects which one cannot forsee. This really applies to all meditation. It is well known, for instance, that the spiritual exercises of St. Ignatius of Loyala are so exhausting that certain people have to be sent away or are only given the exercises in a mitigated form.[83] Another aspect of the same problem is very evident in the lives of the Brontë sisters, who gave most of their en-

---

[81] *Two Essays on Analytical Psychology,* CW 7, pars. 322f.

[82] Ibid., par. 336.

[83] The answers in these exercises, however, are already more or less fixed by the dogma, whereas in conversations with the animus the idea is to let him answer with no restrictions.

ergy to the inner world and were correspondingly weakened in the outer.[84]

It is true that a modern woman—who faces her unconscious because her life is disturbed by knowing too little of her own mind or animus—is in a very different position from the Brontës. Nevertheless, it cannot be emphasized too much that the technique of active imagination should be used with the utmost seriousness or not at all. Moreover, a relationship to the analyst, or to someone else who will understand and provide a hold in the outer world, is indispensable. Perhaps fortunately, most of us have the greatest resistances to using it. Very few people touch it unless they are forced to do so. Most people think they are inventing the whole thing or else they are afraid of it from the beginning. Some people indeed seem to use it with a sort of fatal facility; they can produce fantasies by the dozen without—as far as one can see—it having any direct effect on them at all. This is probably because they do not give themselves actively to it and therefore it remains ineffective, both in a positive and negative sense.[85]

The form of active imagination which Jung describes in the passages quoted above—allowing one's "invisible partner" a voice—requires a lot of practice. One must learn, for instance, to put a question actively and then to be completely passive until the answer comes of itself. After a bit, the answers are usually so far from what one could think of consciously, that the idea that one invents the reply disappears of itself. But again it is dangerous if one takes the answers for gospel. One must always try to find out who is speaking and, when the conversation is over, weigh it very carefully, like any conversation with another person. In this way, it is my experience that one can learn things of the greatest value about one's animus, and also, of course, more than incidentally, about other figures if they appear; moreover, this method is the best one I know for really coming to terms with the unconscious.[86]

One day, a woman who did a good deal of active imagination was talk-

---

[84] [See Barbara Hannah, "Victims of the Creative Spirit."—Ed.]

[85] Examples of a passive and active attitude toward fantasy can be found in the chapter on "The Technique of Differentiation Between the Ego and the Figures of the Unconscious," in Jung's *Two Essays,* CW 7, pars. 341ff.

[86] By "this method" I mean active imagination in general. The usual form—in which the woman watches her animus objectively and learns to take a hand in the game herself—is at least equally effective. Some women prefer to do things silently with their animus, just feeling his presence and so on. The important thing is to find the way which suits the individual.

ing to her animus, when to her great surprise he suddenly remarked: "You and I are in a most awfully difficult position. We are linked together like Siamese twins and yet belong to totally different realities. You know, your reality is just as invisible and ghostlike to me as mine is to you." She admitted that she had never thought of that before. She had naively assumed that he saw everything in our reality as we do ourselves. In fact, some of his interference had given her the impression that he saw it a good deal too clearly and that this was why he could so frequently outwit her!

The woman then asked him: "But if our reality is so insubstantial to you, why do you so often interfere?" He replied: "If you leave something undone, I am forced to intervene. But I can quite understand that in terms of your world it may often be beside the mark."

Jung has pointed out that when the animus interferes in our daily life, it is usually in a place where we have not given the matter our fullest conscious consideration, particularly where we fail in the realm of feeling. But it seems to me that the remark about the two realities is very enlightening. It shows us, for instance, that the animus is just as much in need of information from us about our reality as we are from him about his reality. Moreover, just as he can help us in the invisible world of the collective unconscious so, evidently, we can help him in our reality. We also see here why it was so dangerous for the woman with the animus she called Archibald to consult him about all the details of her daily life.

We find the same idea in another form in a most interesting series of dreams and fantasies which Emma Jung presents and interprets in the second part of her book on the animus.

This animus, which appeared in the first dream as a bird-headed monster with a bladderlike body, begins to lose its dangerous and destructive character in a dream where he is living on the moon as the ghostly lover of a human girl. She must take him a blood sacrifice each new moon, though in between she may live freely on the earth as a human being. As the new moon approaches, the ghostly lover turns her into a beast of prey and, as this brute, she is forced to bring the sacrifice to her lover. Through the sacrifice, however, the ghostly lover himself is turned into a sacrificial bowl which, like the Uroborus, devours and renews itself.

In a later fantasy, this same animus, whose name interestingly enough is Amandus (literally, "to be loved"), entices the girl to enter his house, gives her wine and takes her into a cellar with the purpose of killing her.

The girl is suddenly seized with a kind of ecstasy, throws her arms round the murderer in a loving embrace which robs him of his power, so that, after promising to stand by her in the future as a helpful spirit he dissolves into air. Emma Jung points out that the ghostly power of the moon bridegroom is broken by the blood sacrifice (i.e., by the gift of libido), and that of the would-be murderer by the loving embrace.

Since we are dealing as much as possible with the strictly practical side, we should try to translate this into terms of everyday life. What does it mean to give libido and love to the animus? Mrs. Jung makes this very clear: it is giving him energy, time and attention, not only in order to get acquainted with him but also that he may have the opportunity to express his spiritual and mental nature through us. When we give him libido and love, we consciously and intentionally place our faculties at his disposal in order that he may have the means of expressing the values of his reality.

In the first example, the girl is turned into a beast of prey. This is a process that we can observe very clearly both in life and in analysis, as for instance when we spoil an analytic hour by getting into the animus and letting him twist everything until it is all just beside the point and we are offended, angry and so on. When we go home, the animus goes on tempting us: the analyst should not have said this or that, he does not understand, he has a preference for so-and-so and probably she has poisoned him against us, and so on. If we give in to these ideas, it will not be long before we are completely identical with our emotions, that is, with our passionate shadow who, in her turn, is identical with our animal nature. The animus opinions have turned us into a beast of prey. But if we admit and know that we let the animus catch us (in this case that we have lost the hour and made a nuisance of ourselves, if not worse), we suffer the penalty and thus, by our suffering, give the blood which can transform the animus.

It is essential in such a situation to realize that it was the animus and his opinions that spoiled the hour, against the wish of the conscious ego, or nothing at all will be gained. The animus, it is true, will always turn the tables very neatly and—if he fails in his endeavor to make a woman blame the analyst, husband or whoever it may be—he will attempt to throw the whole blame on the woman herself. If she believes him, she will get into a state of inferiority which is just as destructive as her emotion and rage. This blaming of a woman for all that he does himself is one of his best trump cards, for he thus binds her to his own existence and the thing for which she can really be blamed: failure to know her own animus. In his untransformed state, we may always reckon with the fact that he is trying to get us back into the fold of Mother Nature, and to prevent any escape from the old order. And we also are very reluctant to leave the false security which pervades an unconscious state of possession.

We talk a lot about love of freedom, it is true, but this love is inclined to be rather superficial and lukewarm. We also love avoiding responsibility, particularly inner responsibility. It is pleasant to be convinced that we know what to do, and no one is more convincing on this point than the animus, and if once we give up accepting his guidance unquestioningly we shall find ourselves in constant doubt. Doubt is very laming to the young, but as Jung often remarked, in later life it is the beginning of wisdom. Extreme certainty in the animus, indeed, is always a sign that only one side of him is constellated, for his real dual nature forms a most painful paradox. Enduring this paradox is one of the chief ways in which we can give the "blood" which can transform the animus.

An experience such as mentioned above, when the animus has twisted what has been said until it is all just beside the mark, is often an excellent opportunity to begin a conversation with him. We must keep an extremely open mind, however, for his logos principle is the direct opposite to relationship, and his interference, though quite wrong from our point of view, may be logical and even right from his. These conversations, therefore, are quite as difficult as any conversation in the outer world and demand a total effort, for we must both see his point of view and stand firm in our own.

The Animus in a Human Life

In order to get a real idea of the practical side of the animus, we must see him at work day to day. I have taken the material for this purpose from a very strange document belonging to the second half of the sixteenth century. It concerns the case of a nun, called Jeanne Fery, who was possessed at a very early age and subsequently successfully exorcised. Part of the document is autobiographical; the girl herself describes her experiences while she was possessed. The remainder is an account of the end of the case—including the long and weary process of exorcism—signed by a lawyer in the presence of the Archbishop of Cambrai, various confessors, doctors and other eye-witnesses, including many of the sisters in the convent where Jeanne was a nun. Unfortunately, I have not yet been successful in obtaining a copy of the original document, but it is reported in Joseph Görres, *Die Christliche Mystik.*[87] This is, of course, a great disadvantage, but I have checked a good many of the reports given by Görres with the originals in the "Acta Sanctorum" and, though not infallible, I have found him reliable.[88]

Görres goes into considerable detail but I can only give a short overview of the case and then briefly point out the resemblances between Jeanne's spirits and the animus as we know him today. This case was evidently very famous in its day. Two editions of the report were printed at Paris in 1586 and it was translated and printed in German in 1589.

Jeanne Fery was born about 1559 at Sore, on the Sambre, and later became a nun in a convent of Black Sisters at Mons en Hainaut, in the diocese of Cambrai. Her report begins with the statement that she knows it was the curse of her father which delivered her over to the devil. (She evidently had a very bad relation to him, what we should call a negative father complex.) She goes on to say that the devil appeared to her when she was four years old, in the shape of a handsome young man who offered to become her father. As he gave her white bread and apples, she accepted his suggestion and came to regard him as her real father. While she was a child, there were two of these father figures and the second always prevented her from feeling the strokes when she was beaten. This lasted until she was twelve years old when, tired of the convent where she was being educated, she returned to her mother, who, however, soon sent her away to Mons as an apprentice to a dressmaker.

Here she seems to have been left almost entirely to her own devices and the first young man appeared to her again. He told her that, as she had accepted him as her father, she must now, being no longer a child, renounce her baptism and all the ceremonies of the Christian Church, ratify the ear-

---

[87] Vol. 5, pp. 177ff.

[88] Just before the date on which this manuscript was promised, the photostats of the original French edition arrived from the Bibliotheque Nationale in Paris (Histore Admirable et Veritable des Choses advenues a l'endroict d'une Relieuse professe du convent des Soeurs noires. . ." a Paris, chez Gilles Blaise, Libraire au mont S. Hilaire, a l'image Sainct Catherine, M.D. LXXXVI). There was only time to check very roughly, but I was thus able to confirm my previous impression, that Görres gives a reliable account of the case. The original, however, is considerably longer, and therefore some interesting and subtle facts have been omittted. The whole book would repay further study.

lier agreement and promise to live according to his will. He told her that everybody lived that way although they did not say so. He threatened her with dire punishment if she refused and promised her gold and silver and every delicious food if she accepted. After a short resistance, she agreed to everything and immediately a multitude of spirits appeared and forced her to sign the contract with her blood. (This was a shock to her as she had never seen more than two or at the most three of these figures before.) They then enclosed the agreement in a pomegranate and forced her to eat it. It was marvelously sweet until the last bite, which was more bitter than she could endure.

From that time on, she took a great dislike to the Church—her feet were often so heavy that she could hardly reach the door—but she did not leave it. Her spirits did not insist on her doing so but she had to give them her tongue so that they could control her confessions. Her outer confessions, therefore, were naturally entirely falsified. Interestingly enough, however, she apparently had to confess the exact truth to one of her spirits, particularly concerning any pious action or prayer, for which she was forced to perform severe penance. She was also obliged to take the host out of her mouth at Mass and hide it in her handkerchief, and then, though she tried to keep it in a clean place, it was spirited away. Her spirits taught her to despise everything to do with Christianity, scoffing at a God who could not save himself from the cross. She believed them implicitly, thought Christ worse than the thieves with whom he was crucified, and could no longer understand how people could reverence such a God. They persuaded her to think herself the happiest and most privileged of mortals.

When she entered the convent, she had to sign a new contract giving them both her soul and body forever, and this was repeated again on the night that she took her final vows as a nun. She also had to renounce the Pope and the "evil Archbishop" to whom she had made her vows. The spirit in possession of her tongue made her very bright and witty and, in order not to lose this gift, she gave one spirit her memory, another her reason and a third her will, and, as she says, they thus entered and took up their abode in her, each in his own place. They also took possession of her body, again appearing as a legion of devils for this purpose. The so-called "spirit of blood"—sometimes called the devil or even the god of blood— played a great role in the ceremonies and, as becomes clear in the account of the exorcism, a special devil seems to have taken possession of each part of her body and had to be driven out separately by the Archbishop.

They made her take part in mock communions, held to their own honor, and gave her wonderful food on the days of penance and made her fast during Church festivals. One, whom she liked particularly, seems always to have been with her, but some of them were very cruel to her so that she slowly became less wholehearted in her worship of them, even beginning to think, when devout people praised the sacraments, that, if a sign was vouchsafed her, she might worship Christ as well as her other gods. This made her spirits very angry and they made her take a piece of the host and obliged her to pierce it with a knife. She says that blood flowed from it and the whole room was filled with the bright radiance which surrounded the host. Then she was very frightened, for all her spirits fled with terrible shrieks and she was left alone half dead upon the floor.

She now realized, for the first time, that she had been deceived and, when she thought of the sign that had been granted her, she fell into despair. The spirits then returned and, changing their tune, reproached her for her treatment of the true God, whom they now said was also their God, and told her that her sins would never be forgiven, so that she had better follow the example of Judas Iscariot and hang herself with her leather girdle. She gave it into their hands and told them to hang her if they pleased. But, though they tried to kill her in every way they could, they were always prevented. She also failed, though a crowd of spirits was helping her, to kill herself.

Then a time of great suffering began for Jeanne. Her spirits prevented her from confessing to a priest but, for the first time, the authorities began to notice that she was not what she should be as a Christian and a nun. The matter was taken up by Louis de Berlamont, who was Archbishop and Duke of Cambrai at that time. He took a most active part in her liberation. Though it was her transference to him that eventually freed her, she says that at first the spirits blinded her eyes so that, although she had at once felt an impulse to take refuge with him, he seemed to her severe and terrible. She says that, though the spirits tormented her with the most terrible visions of hell and so on, Mary Magdalene, who appears as her protector, never gave way. She assures us that all this really happened and was no fantasy or imagination.

There are still a few facts which we must take from the other part of the document. We learn there that, although she was exorcised at once, her liberation took two years, entailing the most tremendous efforts on the part of the exorcists, particularly of the Archbishop himself, and of several of the sisters who assisted them in their work. Jeanne's own attitude varied: a vision of Mary Magdalene—who interestingly enough first appeared when she threw herself at the feet of the Archbishop—would strengthen her wish to be freed, but the spirits still had a great deal of power over her.

Most of the time she showed the greatest obstinacy and resistances. Her spirits went on with their advice to commit suicide or, in the language of the time, threw her violently about the room and even out the window. She was always black and blue and her health suffered so severely that, at one time, her doctor said she could not possibly recover. At other times her senses deserted her and she was practically out of her mind. She was taken round to all the sacred relics within reach, bathed in holy water and constantly exorcised.

Slowly the evil spirits had enough of such treatment and departed, all except one—the original father figure. He told her that he had no intention of deserting her and that he had done everything for her, made her witty, intelligent and so on, and that if he left her she would regress to a mere child of four, that is, the age she was when she was first possessed. She, also, was most unwilling to be parted from him and fell at the feet of the exorcists begging them to leave her just this one. When this request was refused, she cried, "Oh what a bitter separation!" and was in complete despair. She only consented when her main exorcist promised her that he would be her father and the Archbishop her grandfather.

When this last spirit had left her, she lay exhausted, a natural, simple child who could only say: "Father, house and pretty Mary." It required repeated blessings from the Archbishop to free her tongue and the other members of her body, and even then she had to be reeducated exactly like a child. A year of penance was then ordered during which her spirits constantly returned and tried to regain possession of her. Mary Magdalene also reappeared several times, always with a strengthening effect. Nevertheless, Jeanne had constant relapses. Once the Archbishop was so violently attacked by the spirits that we are told he was only just able to defend himself and escape with his life.

The final scene is particularly interesting from our point of view. Jeanne asked all the priests and sisters who had been helping her to gather round and then—in the presence of her protecting saint, Mary Magdalene—

began a last fight with her spirits. She held a long conversation with them *herself*. (This is the only case I have met so far where the sufferer does the talking herself. Such conversations are common in the books but usually it is the exorcist who talks to the spirits.) During this conversation, which unfortunately is not reported in detail, she cried out in anguish several times, saying that the spirits were torturing her unbearably, and she also begged for the help of all those present. They prayed for her unceasingly and at last, completely exhausted, she emerged from the fight healed and victorious. Shortly after, Mary Magdalene appeared to her once again and assured her that there would be no return.

*

Perhaps the reader is surprised to find such outlandish material in a paper which claims to be dealing with our own daily contact with the animus. But the people of the sixteenth century still had a naive attitude toward these phenomena, and so described their experiences much more graphically and simply than our modern rational prejudices would ever allow. This is certainly an extreme case—a borderline case as we should call it today—and moreover it is reported from a totally different standpoint to that of modern psychology. But the main facts concerning the nature of the animus agree in all essentials with the facts as we experience them in Jungian psychology today.

As a good many things are reported which border on the so-called supernatural, I should like to quote a short passage from Jung's essay, "Psychology and Religion," where he gives a clear statement on his psychological approach toward such material. He says:

> [My] standpoint is exclusively phenomenological, that is, it is concerned with occurrences, events, experiences—in a word, with facts. Its truth is a fact and not a judgment. When psychology speaks, for instance, of the motif of the virgin birth, it is only concerned with the fact that there is such an idea, but it is not concerned with the question whether such an idea is true or false in any other sense. It is psychologically true inasmuch as it exists. Psychological existence is subjective in so far as an idea occurs in only one individual. But it is objective in so far as that idea is shared by a society—by a *consensus gentium*.[89]

There is no doubt, from the number of witnesses in whose presence the

---

[89] *Psychology and Religion*, CW 11, par. 4.

document was signed, that the report on Jeanne Fery was established by a
consensus gentium. Moreover this is only one of hundreds or even thou-
sands of such reports. Therefore we are concerned with the fact that a large
number of people were convinced of the reality of these phenomena, and
not with the question of whether the supernatural elements in the case actually happened or not.

It seems to me that Jeanne's experiences with her spirits give us an unusually clear picture of how the animus can possess a woman and wrap her
away from the world in a sort of cocoon of fantasies and opinions. But, as
he represents her unconscious mind, he can, at the same time, make her
very intelligent and even witty, so that she can impress her environment
although she cannot relate to it. No one noticed that there was anything
wrong with Jeanne until after the sign from the Host threw her into a violent conflict. It is very difficult for us to realize the extent to which mankind is possessed. A girl like Jeanne might easily escape detection because
she would not seem so very different from many other women!

Of course, when possession has an effect on the environment which
passes a certain degree, as was the case with Hitler, for instance, it is evident to everyone who stands outside the charmed circle. As Jung says in
his essay "Wotan":

> One man, who is obviously "possessed," has infected a whole nation to
> such an extent that everything is set in motion and has started rolling on
> its course towards perdition.[90]

Those words were written in 1936 and were amply borne out by subsequent events. But the fact that such a thing was possible, "in a civilized
country that had long been supposed to have outgrown the Middle Ages,"[91]
is a symptom of our modern state of mind which we cannot afford to over-
look. To put the blame on others is worse than useless, for, by such a
procedure, we shall only forfeit all chance of doing anything about it in
ourselves, and so encourage the whole problem to remain in projection.

Many women would be able to find parallels to Jeanne's childhood experience with her spirits if they looked back thoughtfully on their own
childhood. Some children still escape, when the outer world seems cold and
unsympathetic, into an imaginary world peopled with their equivalent of

---

[90] *Civilization in Transition,* CW 10, par. 388.
[91] Ibid., par. 373.

Jeanne's spirits. This often seems harmless enough and may even bear wonderful fruit in later life, if this inner world is subjected to hard creative work, as in the case of the Brontës. But when it is indulged in too long or is used as a mere escape from the knocks and disappointments of outer life, it severs people, already in their childhood, from relationship to their environment. It attracts a negative animus similar to Jeanne's spirits, outlandish as this language seems to our present rational way of thinking.

Perhaps we can get nearer to understanding if we remember that the animus is a woman's unconscious mind, and that many of his manifestations are thoughts or opinions. Revengeful thoughts, the feeling of being misunderstood or unappreciated, jealous thoughts, a "wait until I have a chance and I will show them" attitude, these are all manifestations of the negative aspect of our unconscious mind, which is lying in wait for us today just as it was in the time of Jeanne Fery.

It is true that Jeanne evidently had unusually few roots in the outside world. Her negative father complex does not seem to have been compensated by the mother, for all we hear about the latter is that she soon sent her away to a considerable distance. Moreover, she evidently took no trouble to see that the girl was looked after, for Jeanne tells us she was left completely free while she lived with the dressmaker.

Right at the beginning we get a hint as to why Jeanne's animus became so completely devilish. She accepted the young man's offer to be her father because he gave her white bread and apples. (There is a great deal about food in her report so she was apparently unusually greedy, which is not surprising when we consider how little love she seems to have received as a child.) In a discussion once at Ascona, Professor Jung pointed out that the animus himself is neither good nor evil, but is a completely dual figure. He only becomes infernal when he hooks onto egotistical demands in the human being. Therefore it was originally Jeanne's greed, and later her wish to be witty and brilliant, to outshine her fellow beings, that constellated the infernal side of her animus. The second figure possessed her because she hated to suffer; he bribed her into admitting him by preventing her from feeling the strokes when she was beaten.

It is interesting that her childish lapses would not have bound her without ratification when she grew up. As I tried to point out in my paper on "The Problem of Women's Plots in *The Evil Vineyard*," there are always recurring moments when we get a chance to change our course, to see what the animus is doing. This ratification would represent such a moment. Jeanne evidently knew already that she was doing wrong, for we hear that she resisted for a time. But her old hunger and fear of punishment prevailed, so she consented to everything. It is interesting that this was directly followed by the appearance of a multitude of spirits ("his name is legion"). In other words, she had ratified her agreement and again offered egotistical hooks, and thus set the seal to a continuance of the infernal aspect of her animus.

To a lesser degree, we can observe the same process in ourselves each time we give way to an animus opinion, for it is immediately followed by a chain of other opinions. Recall our previous example of spoiling an hour with the analyst by animus opinions. Unless we can pull ourselves together and see what we have done, a whole chain of resistances and opinions (the multitude of spirits) will automatically follow and, as we saw, in no time we shall be identical with our animal shadow. That is, we shall be as completely unconscious and possessed by the animus as Jeanne herself.

It is enlightening that, in order to keep her witty tongue, Jeanne had to give up control of her memory, reason and will, each to a separate spirit. Anyone who has had practical experience in the field of analysis will recognize this mechanism. In some cases, it really seems as if what is said is twisted before it reaches the patient's consciousness. This mechanism is particularly clear as regards memory. One often has the feeling that some little demon is constantly at work, taking away the important things and replacing them with inappropriate and meaningless opinions. The language of those days seems to me particularly apt in this respect.

Interestingly enough, it is Jeanne's greed that is both her downfall and the first step toward her recovery. She begins to think she might have Christ as well as her other gods, and asks for a sign. The sign, however, because it comes from the opposite pole, throws her into an unbearable conflict, into all she had been trying to avoid. The spirits then behave in a way that is not characteristic of the animus: they throw over everything they have said before and reproach her for having denied the true God. Here we see how brilliantly the animus can turn the tables when it suits him, and how he can reduce a woman to a hopeless state of inferiority. Such irresponsible blaming for whatever happens, particularly for what he has done himself, is really the hallmark of the animus in his negative aspect.

It seems to me that the most enlightening and certainly the most reassuring thing about the whole case is the intervention of Mary Magdalene, the great sinner and the great lover.[92] Jeanne has to reach complete despair, see herself as Judas Iscariot and try to draw the logical consequence before this figure is constellated. In psychological language, this figure would be a symbol of the Self. It is true that there is no shadow figure in the material: Jeanne was living on the shadow level herself, so that it would in any case be her better qualities which were repressed. Moreover, in the early stages of an analysis, for instance, the figures of the shadow and Self often appear as one.

Mary Magdalene fits the role to perfection. First, she represents the one who sinned and repented or, in psychological language, accepted responsibility for her dark side. Therefore her intervention points to the fact that Jeanne may not take the easy way out; she must see what she has done and take the consequences. Secondly, Mary Magdalene, as the great lover, represents woman's best defense against being possessed by the animus: taking the heart as her guiding principle, listening to her true feelings instead of having opinions about how she ought to feel. (Naturally, typology plays a certain role here, but we have no space to consider this aspect.)

With the intervention of Mary Magdalene, Jeanne can no longer function as a fraud. The approach of any image of the Self always tears away the veils of hypocrisy and illusion and confronts us with what we really are. As a Catholic nun living several hundred years ago, Jeanne was naturally in a very different position from what we should see today. The solution of exorcism, of driving out one opposite in order to cling entirely to the other, may strike us as highly unsatisfactory. But at that time it was the only solution, and even today there are a few cases where people seem to be possessed by alien spirits from the collective unconscious, or by something to which it is impossible for them to relate in any way. I have heard Professor Jung say, in more than one case, that the only thing to be

---

[92] An interesting detail, omitted by Görres, is that it was when Jeanne threw herself at the feet of the Archbishop that Mary Magdalene first appeared in a vision; it recalls Mary herself washing the feet of Christ with her tears and anointing them with the precious ointment (Luke 7:38). This shows us that it was Jeanne's transference to the Archbishop which first released positive and healing forces in her own psyche. Another point omitted by Gorres, which is also of particular interest to our theme, is that her autobiographical account was said to be dictated by Mary Magdalene and was written at one sitting, by what we would call automatic writing

done was to help the patient to lock a certain aspect of the animus away.

The practice of exorcism is today by no means so much on the shelf in Church circles as one is inclined to assume. For instance, the work of the Capuchin monks in this area is well known, at any rate in Switzerland, and much respected. I admit, however, that I was agreeably surprised to learn from his biography that the late Nugent Hicks, Bishop of Lincoln and former Vicar of Brighton, had practiced exorcism himself on more than one occasion. He undoubtedly took the existence of demon-possession exceedingly seriously, as is proved by the fact that he took expert advice concerning the problem of what to do with the spirits after he had cast them out.[93] This puzzle appears again and again in the medieval literature.

Jeanne's transference to the Archbishop undoubtedly played the leading role in her recovery. It is interesting that the positive aspect of the animus only appeared in projection. There is no mention, at any rate by Görres, of Christ or of any male saint. The Archbishop was more or less in the same position as a modern analyst, but of course he met the problem in the contemporary frame of the Church, and thus in a totally different way. It is interesting too that her spirits attacked him, so that he could hardly defend himself, which was always a much dreaded consequence of exorcism.[94] There are certainly parallels today, but I should like to leave this point to the greater experience of men analysts.

The fact that Jeanne herself took such an active role in the final scene of liberation exactly agrees with modern experience. Nothing can be done if the will to be cured is lacking, if the patient herself will not take an active part. Moreover, the fact that Jeanne was now on such terms with the people around her as to be able to ask their collaboration, shows how far she had moved from the witty, intelligent girl who apparently only wished to impress her community. She was sufficiently related to her environment to expose herself in her weakness and had gained sufficient humility to know that the people she despised and wished to outshine were really in a position to help her.

That it is Mary Magdalene who appears and tells Jeanne that she is finally liberated again agrees with our own experience, according to which it

---

[93] See Maurice Headlam, *Bishop and Friend,* pp. 78ff. The Bishop was born in 1872 and died in 1942.

[94] The enormous sacrifices demanded of the Archbishop only became clear to me when I studied the original document.

is only with the help of the Self that we can be freed from the animus in his possessive aspect. The Self represents a unique individual experience but, at the same time, also has a collective aspect in that it reaches far beyond the comprehension or experience of any single person.[95] The animus, on the other hand, although he can represent the principle of individuation, is characterized by a purely collective standpoint. Jung has often pointed out that the animus thinks in terms of the 11,000 virgins! We can see this in our material when the animus tells Jeanne—on the occasion of her signing her first contract with him—that everyone lives that way although they do not say so.

Like all material from the past, the story of Jeanne has mainly a comparative value. It shows us how that age regarded eternal facts which appear ever and again in new clothes. Perhaps the most striking difference is the attitude to the opposites. Presumably a Jungian psychologist would have seen a value in that last spirit, realized his dual nature and known how to help the girl to transform him into a function between conscious and unconscious where, as Jung often says, the animus and anima are in their right place. But in those days the relativity of good and evil was still entirely unrecognized.

The Archetypal Background

In the case of Jeanne Fery we have stripped off a layer of our contemporary rational prejudices and looked at a fragment of a human life in an age when the *consensus gentium* was entirely convinced of the existence of the invisible aspect of life. People of that time experienced the inexorable reality of compelling forces that motivate us with or without our knowledge.

But in order to get a better idea of these forces, their effect on and possibilities for the human being, we should attempt to strip off another layer. We should try to see something of the dual nature of those forces which form the collective archetypal background of each individual psyche. Jung has often pointed out how well we can see this background in the myths and fairy stories which are to be found all over the world, and in this treasure trove we can find the background of our problem portrayed again and again in its innumerable aspects.

We will take just one simple fairy tale to illustrate this point, called

---

[95] See *Psychology and Alchemy,* CW 12, par. 329.

"Die Gansemagd."[96] Marie-Louise von Franz was kind enough to draw my attention to this story which suits our purpose particularly well, as the role of the shadow—which was missing in the case of Jeanne Fery—is especially well portrayed.[97]

Once upon a time there was an old queen who had been a widow for many years. She had one beautiful, dearly loved daughter who was betrothed to a king's son at a distant court. When the time came, the queen prepared a rich dowry for her daughter and decided to send her to her wedding on a talking horse, called Falada,[98] with a maid to look after her. Before the princess started, the mother cut her own finger and gave the girl a white cloth with three drops of blood upon it, telling her to preserve it well, for she would need it on the journey.

The day was hot and the princess was thirsty, but the maid refused to dismount and fetch her water from a stream. So the princess got down from the horse and drank at the stream herself. The cloth warned her that this would break her mother's heart if she knew, but the girl was modest and hated to assert herself. The second time this happened, she dropped the cloth and it was carried away by the stream. Then the maid rejoiced, for the princess had lost her only protection. The maid then obliged her to exchange horses and clothes, and she could only buy her life by promising never to reveal what had happened. So the maid married the prince and the real princess was sent to mind the geese with a pert little boy called Kürdchen (Little Conrad).

The maid was afraid that the talking horse would give her away, so she persuaded the prince that Falada should be killed. The real princess bribed the butcher to nail Falada's head in a dark gateway through which she drove the geese every morning and evening. Then they came to the field where she combed her golden hair, and Kürdchen always tried to steal some hairs. But she sang to the wind and asked it to blow away his cap so that

---

[96] [The English version is "The Goose-Girl," in *The Complete Grimm's Fairy Tales,* no. 89, pp. 404ff.—Ed.]

[97] Dr. von Franz is our expert on fairy tales at the C.G. Jung Institute, Zurich. I should like to express my gratitude to her, for she has taught me practically all that I know concerning this theme.

[98] The origin and meaning of this name are unknown, but, according to J. Bolte and G. Polioka (in *Anmerkungen zu den Kinder und Hausmärchen der Brüder Grimm,* vol. 2, p. 274), the different versions of this horse's name prove that it was a horse and not a mare.

he should not return until her hair was finished.

At last Kürdchen got so angry about all this that he went to complain to the old king. When the latter had concealed himself and heard the girl talk to Falada's head and saw that the wind obeyed her, he sent for her but she refused to explain because of the promise which had saved her life. He found out, however, by a trick and also tricked the false bride into devising her own punishment. So the real princess became the prince's wife, and the maid was put naked into a barrel of nails and was dragged through the streets by two white horses until she died.

As Dr. von Franz always points out in her lectures on fairy tales and myths, one cannot take the characters directly as pieces of an individual's psychology. They are rather archetypal, basic structural elements of the collective unconscious and anticipations of the individual elements. From this standpoint, the princess would represent a kind of prototype or archetypal foundation of the ego, the maid of the shadow, Kürdchen of the animus in his infantile, irresponsible aspect, the prince of the animus in his positive aspect, and so on.

The princess has grown up at the court of the queen, that is, in the realm of the eros principle. We hear that her father had long been dead and the only suggestion of the male principle in the original condition is to be found in the talking horse, Falada. In other words, instinct and animus are entirely undifferentiated and appear as one and the same. She must travel a long distance on this contamination of instinct and animus in order to find the prince, her counterpart and true animus, and to enter the realm of logos, reigned over by the old king.

The mother queen sends her forth richly equipped with dowry—that is, with all the gifts and talents she could bestow upon her—and also with the maid, her shadow, originally in its right place, as her servant and follower. But the mother—as an experienced woman, a riper personality—knows that this *transitus* from one principle to its opposite will be fraught with danger. She takes a small knife, a symbol of the logos principle to which the girl is journeying, and wounds herself with it. She thus, through sacrifice and pain, provides her daughter with three drops of the juice of life, of the essence of the heart, of feeling, as an elixir to protect her in all the dangers she may meet.

I should like to remind you here of the great power which the blood spirit had over Jeanne Fery—even calling himself a god—but in that case it was a symptom that the animus had invaded the very citadel of the eros principle. Here, on the contrary, the blood is in its right place and comes from the body of the mother. In this connection, it is also interesting to remember that it was by the help of Mary Magdalene, the great lover, that Jeanne was first able to resist her spirits and to begin the work of liberating herself from their domination.

The trouble with the shadow first begins when the princess does not insist on the maid fetching the water from the stream,[99] while she still had the blood-sprinkled cloth and was in a position to do so. We can observe the same weakness in ourselves each time we do not take full responsibility for what we are or what the situation demands. We take the path of least resistance, as the princess did when she fetched the water herself rather than assert herself and keep the maid in her right place. But we forget that we thus lose a piece of ourselves, which then falls into the power of the unconscious, in this case of the shadow. This lowers our consciousness, as it did that of the princess. The next time our attention wanders at the critical moment and we lose our elixir, our protection against the predominance of the shadow, as the princess lost the blood-sprinkled cloth. This protection is beautifully symbolized here by the drops of blood coming from the very heart of the eros principle.

When the princess has lost this guide, this connection with the leading principle of woman, she has delivered herself into the hands of her shadow. She has given away the key to her position, and it follows, as the night the day, that she must give everything else that she possesses—her dowry, her clothes and even her most valuable instinct and animus—into the hands of her shadow, who then takes over the leading role and reduces the prototype of the ego to the rank of her maid. The princess then does the only thing she can do to save her life: she humbly accepts the role of servant and promises never to tell anyone what has happened.

When we have allowed the shadow to take over the reins, by neglecting the things we ought to have done, we can only follow the example of the princess and practice the virtue of complete humility. We must see what we have done and accept the consequences, on the same principle that, in

---

[99] This water represents the water of life. It is only when one approaches life that the shadow is constellated. While we keep out of it, it is possible to keep our integrity and innocence, but life constellates the whole personality which includes the shadow.

order to regain control of a skidding car, we must steer with the skid at first. There is no hope of regaining control over our shadow if we make matters worse by refusing to see what has happened. The princess is wise enough to accept the situation. She has behaved like a little goose and she uncomplainingly becomes a "goose-girl." Her situation, however, is now very bad. The animus and the shadow are married which, as we saw, is the worst thing that can happen, and even her friendly instinct, Falada, is sent to the butcher.

The archetypal situation portrayed here is one which is frequently set in motion when a woman loses the game to her shadow. The shadow not only marries the animus but destroys the woman's instinct as well, and all that the princess, as the prototype of the ego, can rescue is the head.[100] The head in this case represents above all the natural mind, a kind of inexorable, ruthless truthfulness which exists in every woman although she usually prefers to turn a deaf ear toward it. (This is the mind mentioned earlier as Christina Alberta's "court of conscience" and as the parrot Old Nick in *Green Dolphin Country.*) The fact that the princess rescued this mind and allowed it to speak to her daily was her heroic action which in the end saved the situation. Many a woman's whole life depends on whether she can take this opportunity or not, for this is the inner voice that knows who she is and that will never allow her to deceive herself.

Every morning as the princess drives her geese under the dark gateway—that is, the darkest and saddest place in her *via dolorosa*—she greets Falada's head and expresses her regret that he must hang there. He hails her as "young queen" and reminds her that her mother's heart would break if she knew what had happened. In other words, he confronts her with her sin of taking the path of least resistance, and reminds her that her humility as goose-girl is no final solution. He thus faces her with her whole reality, which—as Jung emphasizes in *Psychology and Alchemy*[101]—is the thing we fear the most.

We are specially told that the princess was very humble and therefore hated to assert herself with the maid. But she cannot leave her opposite qualities, pride and worldly ambition, in the hands of her shadow or they will inevitably destroy her. She must remember who she is and take re-

---

[100] Talking to a head is a well-known archetypal motif; Wotan and Mimir's head, for instance.

[101] CW 12, par. 330.

sponsibility for her position or she will break her mother's heart: murder the very essence of her being and of the feminine eros principle.

This fairy story shows us a very beautiful piece of the archetypal foundation of the whole invaluable technique of conversing with our animus. If we can get things straight with our own unconscious, if we can reach the inner truth, it will often radiate into the outer world and set things straight there, in a way that we could never reach by outer means.

When the princess has passed through the dark gateway of suffering and allowed the voice of truth to reach her, she has gathered sufficient strength to meet the further trials of the day unflinchingly. She must herd her geese, that is, keep those fluttering and militant animals together, see that they can get their food and not allow any of them to stray. Geese are frequently associated with negative mother goddesses and with witches in myths and fairy tales. They are connected with Nemesis, for instance, the goddess of fate, and with the Russian arch-witch, Baba Yaga. The princess, through losing the blood-sprinkled cloth, has lost her connection with the positive mother figure. Therefore she must naturally now become the servant of a negative mother figure and herd her geese.

The action of combing her hair combines some aspects of the same idea. In this case, her hairs would represent her thoughts, and Kürdchen— as the infantile and irresponsible animus—naturally does everything he can to get her thoughts (hairs) into his power and to use them for his own ends, that is, to fill her with animus opinions. She lost the game to her shadow on her journey to her positive animus, and she must now deal with him in a less favorable aspect. But because she is in touch—through her conversations with Falada—with the forces of nature, the wind helps her and blows away Kürdchen's cap every morning, so that he has to attend to his own affairs and she can arrange her thoughts in peace and unmolested.

The wind is perhaps the most primordial image that exists for the spirit per se,[102] and here again we get a wonderful glimpse into the archetypal background of our problem. We see that the negative, infantile, teasing animus, Kürdchen, is powerless against the spirit itself and that, if we can reach these depths in our psyche, we can reach powers that can help us when we are unable to help ourselves. If the princess, as prototype of the

---

[102] To mention only one well-known example: "the rushing mighty wind" that preceded the cloven tongues of fire when the spirit entered the apostles at Pentecost. (Acts 2:2ff)

ego, had relied on rational and conscious means, she could only have quarreled with Kürdchen and he would certainly have been able to obtain some of her hairs. This shows us that direct confrontation with the animus is often unwise and would only result in opinions and a hopeless feeling of defeat. It gives us some idea of the total effort which is required on the long path of reaching a *modus vivendi* with our animus.

It is interesting that it is just Kürdchen, when he is defeated in his plans, who makes the matter known at the court of the king and thus indirectly brings about the solution. The dual role of the animus shows particularly clearly here. If the princess had given way to this teasing, childish, foolish aspect of her animus and allowed him to steal her hair, she would have been in the same position as Jeanne Fery at the beginning of her possession when she, apparently harmlessly, accepted the apples and white bread from the father figure. The princess would thus have taken the first step on the road to becoming a Jeanne Fery, and, if she had not resisted the apparently harmless, if teasing Kürdchen, he would soon have taken on a more negative and finally even an infernal aspect. But, as she stands her ground, Kürdchen is obliged to apply to a higher authority and the positive side of the animus begins to come into play.

This gives us some idea of the vital issues which lie concealed behind the apparently unimportant matter of the thoughts which pass through our mind as we go about our daily life. Every time we give way to an animus opinion, we are allowing our Kürdchen to steal a hair and are moving, imperceptibly but surely, in the direction of Jeanne Fery. Whereas each time we can think of a way of preventing this theft—of resisting the insinuating animus opinion—we move a step nearer to the solution which is waiting for us all, as it was for the princess, although of course in a completely different form for each individual.

When the king had tested Kürdchen's statements by concealing himself and listening to the girl's conversation with Falada, and had seen the wind grant her request, he sent for the goose-girl and asked her to tell him her story. This also gives us a valuable hint as to our dealings with our shadow side. A great many people make the mistake of believing that one can integrate the shadow by living out its qualities. But this mistake leads only to identification with the shadow; we change roles, so to speak, and nothing is gained. But by keeping faith with the shadow, as the princess does here, we grant it the right to exist and pay our debt to it, for, after all, the maid had spared the princess's life when she had it in her power to destroy her utterly.

The king then persuaded the princess to creep into the iron stove and to tell it her troubles. The stove here represents the mother's womb, into which she must creep for rebirth, or the alchemical stove where the process of transformation takes place. Here the princess may speak, for she lays her fate in the hands of the Self so that it, and not the ego, may decide. She also submits to transformation so that the king—who has listened through a pipe—can now reestablish her in the royal rank to which she was born. He has her dressed in royal clothes and arranges the wedding feast so that at last, after much tribulation and error, she reaches the positive animus figure in the person of the king's son.

The false bride, the shadow, sits on the king's other side at the feast and pronounces her own punishment under the impression that she is condemning someone else. The shadow thus overreaches herself and has to submit to being depotentiated. She is dragged naked in a barrel through the streets until she is dead,[103] that is, reduced to an inanimate shadow that follows the ego as the ordinary shadow follows the body. But the princess, as the bride of the king's son, must now take on the responsibility for who she is and not allow her naturally retiring disposition to mislead her again into playing only a portion of her role.

Conclusion

This fairy story has shown us an infinitesimal fragment of the inexhaustible combinations and possibilities which lie concealed in the archetypal foundation of every individual life. As Jung says in his epilogue to "The Psychology of the Transference":

> The series of pictures [from the "Rosarium Philosophorum"] that served as our Ariadne thread is one of many, so that we could easily set up several other working models which would display the process of transference each in a different light. But no single model would be capable of fully expressing the endless wealth of individual variations which all have their *raison d'être.*[104]

---

[103] This motif shows a difference between the archetypal events in fairy tales and individual cases. Archetypes never really die, so the death of an archetypal figure means transformation.

[104] *The Practice of Psychotherapy,* CW 16, par. 538.

The same applies to any story that one may attempt to use as an "Ariadne thread" in the problem of contact with the animus. The "endless wealth of individual variations"—which each of us meets in our negotiations with the animus—are so inexhaustible that it would have been a hopeless task, in a paper of this length, to show him at work in the life of a modern individual, to say nothing of the long case history which would also have been indispensable. Moreover, archetypal material has one great advantage over personal material. We all have the same archetypal background although it is constellated in a different way in every case, whereas there is always a great temptation to identify with other people's personal material and thus to take things out of their context and to interpret them incorrectly.

I should like, finally, to return for a moment to our own age, and give you a fragment of a modern dream which shows the same problem in new clothes. It is part of an interesting series which illustrates the conflict between the collective point of view of the animus and the intensely personal standpoint of the shadow. It is worth mentioning that the dreamer was not in analysis, which means that the material is more naive and complete.

This dreamer was constantly torn in two in her dreams between an inexorable severe animus, who usually appeared as a monk or a priest, and a passionate infantile shadow who appeared as a child or an excitable emotional woman. On the one side she had to accept all the remonstrances of the just but inexorable animus; on the other, she had to lower herself to the level of the shadow against the express orders of the priest. In the dream from which I am taking the following, she was obliged to remain standing in the presence of the priest but nevertheless sank down onto a bench beside the despairing woman. She says that she did not forget her clearly realized obligation to remain standing, nor did she act from defiance, but she was compelled by a compassion greater than herself to sit down beside this woman. She then looked at the priest and there was mercy in his face, but she knew he would punish her severely for what she had done.

When the tension was at its height, she found herself in a great cathedral with the priest behind her and the woman she had befriended in front of her. They were all waiting for something, evidently for some sort of judgment or decision. At last a voice was heard coming from behind and above the priest. This voice was as majestic as the cathedral itself and they all listened in fear and gladness. The voice was full of compassion and yet the judgment was severe. If the child (or passionate woman) recovered from her wounds, the dreamer might go her way in peace, but if not . . . . The dreamer could not hear the alternative but the inference was that it was a sentence of death. Severest justice was thus tempered with mercy in a way which could be accepted by them all.

I need add little to this wonderful dream which shows us how ego, animus and shadow must *all* sacrifice themselves to the will of the Self. But the first sacrifice must come from the side of the ego; it must make conscious all its egotistical demands hitherto projected into the shadow, for, as Jung points out in "Transformation Symbolism in the Mass," we can only sacrifice the things we have.[105] It is only if we are willing to make the utmost sacrifice ourselves that we can hope to move our animus to sacrifice his autonomy and autocratic power over us, and to lower himself to become a function between conscious and unconscious, subservient to the voice that comes from behind and above him, the voice of the uniter of opposites, whether we call it God or the Self.

---

[105] *Psychology and Religion,* CW 11, pars. 376ff.

Appendix
Some Memories of Barbara Hannah

Andrea B. Dykes

The thing I valued most from my contact with Barbara Hannah was the way she was able, right from the start, to make the unconscious a living reality for me. This was undoubtedly because she had experienced it so profoundly herself. It came across in everything she said, whether she was speaking of the inner or outer world. I had had the animus drummed into me by no less than three different analysts in England. Yet it and all the other manifestations of the unconscious remained no more than lifeless theorizing until Miss Hannah set to work on me. I had been seeing her for only two weeks when the reality of the animus hit me like a bolt from the blue—"Oh, *that* is what she means!"

From then on I began to realize more and more the importance of being in touch with the unconscious for the conduct of the whole of life. This is something for which I cannot be sufficiently grateful, and it is the reason why I would certainly choose to analyze with her were I entering upon analysis now. She showed me that the task of working with and on the unconscious is a process which should continue after the actual analysis is finished. Her attitude toward dreams was quite unlike anything I had previously encountered. There was no censure for negative or regressive ones but simply an effort to discover just why they were so bad. This was of the greatest assistance in helping me to overcome the awful feelings of guilt left over from earlier analytic attempts.

She helped me develop my ability to do active imagination by her encouragement and reassurance that my early efforts were in fact genuine and not, as I used to fear, "inventions" on my part. She also instilled in me its importance as a real support in times of trial and crisis.

Of all her books I like *Striving Toward Wholeness* best, especially her treatment of Mary Webb's *Precious Bane,* where she displays an exceptional insight into deeper levels of the feminine psyche. The whole book displays a fresh and original approach to her subject which puts it in a totally different category from the usually forced Jungian interpretation of works of literature.

My strongest impressions of Miss Hannah as a person, not as an analyst, are of her amazing capacity to be absolutely herself in a totally unself-conscious manner, without reference to the image of herself in the psychological world. She was wholly contained within the framework of her own being.

To mention just two of my memories: On one occasion she drove to Kandersteg for a holiday and took me and three other analysands as far as the Brünig Pass. From there we were to find our way back by train. Enroute she gave us lunch at a hotel. As I watched her sitting at the head of the table, I felt she was in truth the Mother Goddess smiling on her children. It was one of the very warmest moments of my entire life. I also recall how, many years later, she was on vacation when the district where I lived was struck by a devastating summer hailstorm. Two days later I received a letter of deepest sympathy for the dreadful damage she realized it must have caused to my beloved garden, and giving me the address of a good garden center where she thought I might be able to find replacements for some of my destroyed plants, late in the season though it was. At that time she was having a holiday and was very busy catching up with her own affairs, yet she wrote to me immediately when she read about the storm in the paper. This was typical of her concern on the human as well as the analytical level for those who worked with her.

Andrea B. Dykes is a Diplomate of the Zurich Jung Institute, and a Training Analyst with the Association of Jungian Analysts, London. She translated The Grail Legend *by Emma Jung and Marie-Louise von Franz.*

Joseph L. Henderson

Barbara Hannah and I arrived in Zurich to enter analysis with C.G. Jung the same year, 1929. Years later Barbara recalled this while introducing me to someone by saying, "Joe and I were psychological babies together." During that first year we lived in the same place (I was going to say "nursery"), the Pension Neptun on Seestrasse, and sat at the same table with two analysands of Toni Wolff: Dr. George Draper of New York and Mrs. James Cabot, a society woman from Boston.

It would be hard to imagine a more unlikely group to sit together day after day, but, due to our common interest, that of being new in Jungian analysis, it worked very well. We laughed a lot and shared choice episodes from our dream life and, thanks to Catherine Cabot's witty associations derived from the pleasure-seeking milieu in which she had grown up in Philadelphia and Europe, we avoided taking ourselves too seriously most of the time. We were unfailingly encouraged in this by Dr. Draper. Some of the other analysands at the Pension Neptun, by contrast, seemed rather gloomy. But I began to suspect, and I am sure Barbara did, too, that they were a bit closer to those regions of the unconscious from which essential insights are perceived. In time our extraverted friends became something of a liability to any deepening process, although we did still enjoy their company.

At length I decided we were all getting a bit too incestuous in our intimate self-revelations, so I left to go to the Dolder Hotel in a different part of Zurich, on the hill overlooking the lake and the mountains. I do not recall how long Barbara stayed there or whether she left too, but we continued to see each other at Jung's English seminar every Wednesday morning for the remainder of that year. I remember her as a deeply introverted person who showed very little of her true self to others. But since I was also a pretty shy member of this seminar of older people, I could hardly have encouraged her to be more open.

In subsequent visits to Zurich during the 1930s I always saw Barbara and enjoyed her wonderful sense of loyalty to her friends and her bracing English sense of humor. Cary Baynes, who with her husband Dr. Godwin Baynes, had translated Jung's early books into English (and later went on to translate Richard Wilhelm's version of the *I Ching),* provided a social center in her house at Kilchberg which we English-speaking people all enjoyed. During this period, my English fiancée, Helena Cornford, came to stay with Cary, and our friendship with Barbara and this group became increasingly important to us as we moved toward marriage.

World War Two marked a sad hiatus in my connection with Jung and our Zurich friends, but when I did return in 1948 for a visit I had a wonderful experience of rediscovery. An outstanding memory of that time was the change I saw in Barbara Hannah, who had been transformed from an earnest but distinctly amateur Jungian into a professional with a whole new capacity for extraversion never expected of her. This change is given its rightful recognition in her own words in her book *Jung: His Life and Work,* but in the early 1950s it bore fruit in her highly articulate seminars and lectures at the newly formed Jung Institute, some of which she also gave to us in San Francisco on one of her trips to America. I remember chiefly the one called "Conversations of a World Weary Man with his Ba," and also her interpretations of the Brontë novels.

From that time on my contacts with Barbara became less personal and we were more like colleagues, meeting only at conferences of one sort or another. It was a pleasure to see her again in the United States at the Second Bailey Island Conference on the occasion of Esther Harding's eightieth birthday, and again that same summer in Zurich. But nothing could quite replace the enjoyment of the years when, as analysands, we felt we belonged to a smaller family of Jungians. At the end of that time I recall the most memorable thing she ever said to me. It was to the effect that the people who patiently continue their analysis with no end in sight are the ones who come out best, in contrast to those who terminate too soon out of expediency or resistance. Judging from her own experience, this did not mean dependency on the analyst or failure to resolve a transference but a genuine transformation in the individuation process. In turn this opened the way to her life work as an analyst. So in recent years I feel I have known her best, in a new way, and renewed our friendship through patients of hers who later worked with me.

Joseph L. Henderson was a founding member of the C.G. Jung Institute of San Francisco, former vice-chairman of the International Association for Analytical Psychology, co-author with Jung of Man and His Symbols, *and author of several books, including* Thresholds of Initiation, Cultural Attitudes in Psychological Perspective, *and* Shadow and Self.

Morton T. Kelsey

I first met Barbara Hannah during the Whitsuntide term of the Zurich Jung Institute in 1955. Max Zeller had arranged for me to have intensive analysis with two different analysts—Barbara Hannah and Franz Riklin. The analysis required five hours a week: two different hours with Dr. Riklin, one two-hour session with Barbara Hannah, and another one-hour session with her. The work with both of them was fascinating, and one of the most helpful things was to discover that both gave me much the same interpretation of dream material with no interaction between them. It was a tremendously validating experience.

I preferred Barbara Hannah's analytical contact to her lecturing style, although I enjoyed both. She was incredibly insightful and very direct at times. It was she who first showed me how to involve myself in real active imagination rather than simply allowing the unconscious to flow in whatever way it chose, and this practice has been remarkably helpful during the years that followed. However, I had to make my own use of Christian symbols as she was either not willing, or did not think it wise, to help me in that direction.

One of her most practical remarks was that if I did not cease my hectic working schedule, I would not live past fifty. This gave me pause for thought. I went home and arranged to have two days off from my busy ministerial schedule. She also showed me what it was to be kind to myself. One time I came in with a bad stomach ache and told her that I had eaten too many sausages because I really could not afford a good meal. She laughed and said, "If you can spend $3500 to come to Zurich and work here, you can certainly spend a little more to get yourself a good meal!" Later, when I took a trip to Liechtenstein and then to Feldkirke, I treated myself to the best meal in the restaurant; it was cordon bleu. This began a whole new way of treating myself kindly.

At times I felt she was not sympathetic to the Church and did not see the value of a genuine religious experience or faith regarding or surrounding the Christ figure. However, I can honestly say that my relationship with her was a turning point in my life, both in learning to do active imagination, in dealing with my dreams, and in treating myself as a human being who could set limits on his activities. I really wonder what my life might have been had I not worked with her. What a tremendous experience she provided as well as a whole new direction.

One of the most important dreams I had was of building Byzantine churches. Both Miss Hannah and Franz Riklin realized, as I did, that the dream was speaking about my own religious background and the need to integrate Greek thought into modern theology. Whereas many of my good friends at the Institute were leaving their former professions, all indications pointed to my going back to mine as a minister. I felt directed to bring the insights of Greek thought and theology, as well as depth psychology, into the Christian framework in which I found myself. This has always been the direction of my life.

Morton T. Kelsey did graduate work at the Episcopal Theological School, Princeton Theological School and the Zurich Jung Institute. He has lectured widely throughout the United States, Europe and the Orient, and is the author of more than two dozen books.

Helen M. Luke

It is thirty years or more since I met Barbara Hannah in Los Angeles, where she had come to lecture on *Confessions of a Justified Sinner,* written by the Scottish author, James Hogg (1770-1835). It was a lecture I have never forgotten and have often wished it had been recorded.

I had not been in America long. In 1949 I had come from England, sponsored by Dr. Fritz Kunkel and Robert Johnson, whom I had met in Zurich when we both studied there. Robert Johnson and I shared an office for our analysands, but since the various training institutes for analytical psychology were only in their beginnings, we did not hold any formal certificates, and at that time lay analysts without medical degrees were often looked upon with suspicion and were not accepted for study. We had individual friends but we were still barred from the official Los Angeles Institute and felt very much isolated.

We had both met Barbara Hannah in Zurich and had attended her lectures there. When she came to Los Angeles we told her of our feelings. She told us of a visit she once made to a city in the United States where the rejection of lay analysts—even those trained by Jung himself—was particularly troubling to her. She said she had gone back to Zurich and spoken to Jung of her distress about the people who were "pushed out into the dark." He had answered her by telling her not to be concerned about that, because his work would largely be carried on by "people in the dark."

At that time of insecure beginnings, the warmth of Barbara Hannah's understanding and the serenity of her spirit were indeed blessings for which I cannot adequately express my gratitude.

Helen M. Luke analyzed and studied in England and in Zurich in the 1940s. She came to the United States in 1949, practiced in Los Angeles for several years, and then co-founded the Apple Farm Community in Three Rivers, Michigan. She is the author of Woman: Earth and Spirit, The Inner Story, *and* Old Age.

Alfred Ribi

My memory of Barbara Hannah focuses around an observation which I made when I was Director of Studies at the Zurich Jung Institute. At times there were conferences with other analysts. Sometimes the opposites were constellated and deep hostility surfaced. In this situation, Barbara Hannah often stated a baffling truth which no one else dared to utter. Then a moment of silence occurred after which there was a great feeling of relief.

She was able to state a truth with no feeling of hostility connected with her statement. Whenever you state a truth in such a way that it suggests triumphing over your enemy, it only provokes more hostility. In her case, the truth came directly out of the Self. She had had enough dealings with animus plots and her own shadow that no contamination of these archetypes appeared in her statement. This allowed her to state the truth in a way that nobody else could.

From this observation I saw how the Self is a reconciling reality in the psyche. It brings together the opposites, especially when one opposite is contaminated with the shadow. It reveals the dark intrigues and plots involved and brings the victory of truth. This observation was decisive for my understanding of the reality of the Self—the central concept of Jungian psychology.

Although my contribution is small, perhaps it will add to the picture of this unique human being named Barbara Hannah.

Dr. Alfred Ribi secured his M.D. from the University of Zurich where he majored in Psychiatry and Psychotherapy. He is a Diplomate of the Zurich Jung Institute, where he was Director of Studies, 1969-71. He is currently a lecturer and Training Analyst at the Zurich Institute.

William R. Sanford

Most of my memories of Barbara Hannah are related to several different occasions. She lectured in Los Angeles in 1952 on her first visit to America. At one meeting where she lectured on some aspect of the Old Testament, she was quite apologetic for daring to speak on this subject with Dr. James Kirsch, a recognized authority on the Old Testament, in the audience. But she said with some finality, "I am going to do it anyway," and it was a wonderful lecture.

In 1957, when I spent six months in Zurich, I heard Barbara's evening lectures at the Psychological Club, which took place over a period of weeks. She lectured on *Aion,* which at that time had not been translated into English, so she read from the German edition. People crowded to hear her because she was very popular. One evening she showed up with her briefcase and all her paraphernalia (which was wonderful to see) and set them on the table. She searched through her bags but, to her consternation, could not find her glasses. Up from the audience jumped Dr. Riklin, who offered his glasses to her, saying, "Here, try these." They worked beautifully and she used them for the entire evening.

My background is very English although I was not born in England. Because Barbara was English, I had a fantastic camaraderie with her. We got along beautifully although I did not do analysis with her, and we were not intimate friends. I always loved her enormous outbursts—I just thought they were great. She showed such genuine enthusiasm.

[Dr. Sanford's third memory of Barbara Hannah was of her speaking at the Bailey Island Conference in 1968, reported in the introduction to "The Beyond," in The Cat, Dog and Horse Lectures, and 'The Beyond.' *"]*

I have not seen Barbara Hannah since that time although I have had correspondence with her on several occasions. In more recent years I have heard rather sharp criticism of her. This has centered around her identity with Jung, her devotion and allegiance to him at the sacrifice of what we often call "the rest of one's life." When such criticism has been voiced, I have taken this stand: "But see what she has done, what she has produced. These are her children--her books, her lectures, her analytical work." I feel strongly about this. Some people can have marriage and a career but it was Barbara Hannah's fate to express her creativity through her work.

Her book *Striving Toward Wholeness* is very important because the title describes perfectly the individuation process. It is a process, a striving, not a goal which can be reached. I often give this book to clients when they get anxious and want to get going; they want solutions, want to get it over with, but the process cannot be manipulated. Individuation is a process and people need to be reminded of this.

From another source, I once heard of an encounter she had with Jung. She went to him with some abominable problem and asked, "What could one possibly do with this?" Jung is reported to have replied, "When you meet a problem of this kind, you can only take that action by which the devil gets you the least." That is a wonderful statement.

William R. Sanford is a Jungian analyst in Del Mar, California.

Bibliography

The Apocrypha According to the Authorized Version. London, England: Oxford University Press, n.d.

Bolte, J., and Polioka, G. *Anmerkungen zu den Kinder und Hausmärchen der Brüder Grimm.* Leipzig: 1915.

Eckhart, Meister. *Meister Eckhart.* Trans. C. de B. Evans. London: Watkins, 1924.

Görres, Joseph. *Die Christliche Mystik.* Munich: 1589.

Grimm Brothers. *The Complete Grimm's Fairy Tales.* New York: Pantheon Books, 1944.

Hannah, Barbara. *The Cat, Dog and Horse Lectures, and "The Beyond."* Ed. Dean L. Frantz. Wilmette, IL: Chiron Publications, 1992.

_____. *Encounters with the Soul: Active Imagination As Deveoped by C.G. Jung.* Santa Monica, CA: Sigo Press, 1981.

_____. *Jung, His Life and Work: A Biographical Memoir.* New York: G.P. Putnam's Sons, 1976

_____. "On Active Imagination." In *Spring 1953.*

_____. "The Problem of Women's Plots in *The Evil Vineyard.*" Lecture 51. London, England: Guild of Pastoral Psychology, 1946.

_____. *Striving Toward Wholeness.* 2nd ed. Santa Monica, CA: Sigo Press, 1988.

_____. "Victims of the Creative Spirit: A Contribution to the Psychology of the Brontës from the Jungian Point of View." Lecture 68. London, England: Guild of Pastoral Psychology, 1950.

Headlam, Maurice. *Bishop and Friend.* London: Macdonald and Co., 1945.

James, M.R., trans. *The Apocrypha of the New Testament.* London: Oxford University Press, 1924.

Jung, C.G. "Alchemy: The Process of Individuation—Notes on Lectures Given at the Eidgenössische Technische Hochschule, Zürich, 1940-41." In *Modern Psychology,* vol. 5. Ed. Barbara Hannah. Zurich: C. G. Jung Institute, 1960.

_____. *C.G. Jung Speaking* (Bollingen Series XCVII). Ed. Wm. McGuire and R.F.C. Hull. Princeton: Princeton University Press, 1977.

_____. *The Collected Works* (Bollingen Series XX). 20 vols. Trans. R.F.C. Hull. Ed. H. Read, M. Fordham, G. Adler, Wm. McGuire. Princeton: Princeton University Press, 1953-1979.

_____. *Memories, Dreams, Reflections.* Ed. Aniela Jaffé. New York: Pantheon Books, 1961.

_____. *Nietzsche's* Zarathustra: *Notes of the Seminar Given in 1934-1939* (Bollingen Series XCIX). 2 vols. Ed. James L. Jarrett. Princeton: Princeton University Press, 1988.

_____. *The Visions Seminars.* Zurich: Spring Publications, 1976.

Jung, Emma. *Animus and Anima: Two Essays.* Zurich: Spring Publications, 1957.

The Norton Anthology of Poetry. 3rd ed. Ed. Alexander Alison et al. New York: W.W. Norton and Co., 1970.

Rahner, Hugo. "Antenna Crucis, III, The Wooden Ship." In *Zeithschrift für Katholische Theologie,* vol. 66 (1942).

Scharf, Rivkah. *Satan in the Old Testament.* Evanston, IL: Northwestern University Press, 1967.

Stevenson, Robert Louis. *Across the Plains.* New York: Charles Scribner's Sons, 1916.

_____. *Dr. Jekyll and Mr. Hyde.* New York: Bantam Books, 1981.

von Franz, Marie-Louise. *Aurora Consurgens.* New York: Pantheon Books, 1966.

_____. *On Dreams and Death: A Jungian Interpretation.* La Salle, IL: Open Court, 1998.

Wilhelm, Richard, and Jung, C.G.. *The Secret of the Golden Flower: A Chinese Book of Life.* London: Routledge and Kegan Paul, 1931.

Index

Studies in Jungian Psychology
by Jungian Analysts

Quality Paperbacks

Prices and payment in $US (except in Canada, $Cdn)

1. The Secret Raven: Conflict and Transformation
Daryl Sharp (Toronto). ISBN 0-919123-00-7. 128 pp. $16

2. The Psychological Meaning of Redemption Motifs in Fairy Tales
Marie-Louise von Franz (Zürich). ISBN 0-919123-01-5. 128 pp. $16

3. On Divination and Synchronicity: The Psychology of Meaningful Chance
Marie-Louise von Franz (Zürich). ISBN 0-919123-02-3. 128 pp. $16

4. The Owl Was a Baker's Daughter: Obesity, Anorexia and the Repressed Feminine Marion Woodman (Toronto). ISBN 0-919123-03-1. 144 pp. $16

5. Alchemy: An Introduction to the Symbolism and the Psychology
Marie-Louise von Franz (Zürich). ISBN 0-919123-04-X. 288 pp. $20

6. Descent to the Goddess: A Way of Initiation for Women
Sylvia Brinton Perera (New York). ISBN 0-919123-05-8. 112 pp. $16

7. The Psyche as Sacrament: A Comparative Study of C.G. Jung and Paul Tillich John P. Dourley (Ottawa). ISBN 0-919123-06-6. 128 pp. $16

8. Border Crossings: Carlos Castaneda's Path of Knowledge
Donald Lee Williams (Boulder). ISBN 0-919123-07-4. 160 pp. $16

9. Narcissism and Character Transformation: The Psychology of Narcissistic Character Disorders
Nathan Schwartz-Salant (New York). ISBN 0-919123-08-2. 192 pp. $18

10. Rape and Ritual: A Psychological Study
Bradley A. Te Paske (Santa Barbara). ISBN 0-919123-09-0. 160 pp. $16

11. Alcoholism and Women: The Background and the Psychology
Jan Bauer (Montreal). ISBN 0-919123-10-4. 144 pp. $16

12. Addiction to Perfection: The Still Unravished Bride
Marion Woodman (Toronto). ISBN 0-919123-11-2. 208 pp. $18pb/$25hc

13. Jungian Dream Interpretation: A Handbook of Theory and Practice
James A. Hall, M.D. (Dallas). ISBN 0-919123-12-0. 128 pp. $16

14. The Creation of Consciousness: Jung's Myth for Modern Man
Edward F. Edinger (Los Angeles). ISBN 0-919123-13-9. 128 pp. $16

15. The Analytic Encounter: Transference and Human Relationship
Mario Jacoby (Zürich). ISBN 0-919123-14-7. 128 pp. $16

16. Change of Life: Dreams and the Menopause
Ann Mankowitz (Ireland). ISBN 0-919123-15-5. 128 pp. $16

17. The Illness That We Are: A Jungian Critique of Christianity
John P. Dourley (Ottawa). ISBN 0-919123-16-3. 128 pp. $16

18. Hags and Heroes: A Feminist Approach to Jungian Psychotherapy with Couples Polly Young-Eisendrath (Philadelphia). ISBN 0-919123-17-1. 192 pp. $18

19. Cultural Attitudes in Psychological Perspective
Joseph L. Henderson, M.D. (San Francisco). ISBN 0-919123-18-X. 128 pp. $16

20. The Vertical Labyrinth: Individuation in Jungian Psychology
Aldo Carotenuto (Rome). ISBN 0-919123-19-8. 144 pp. $16

44. The Dream Story
Donald Broadribb (Baker's Hill, Australia). ISBN 0-919123-45-7. 256 pp. $20

45. The Rainbow Serpent: Bridge to Consciousness
Robert L. Gardner (Toronto). ISBN 0-919123-46-5. 128 pp. $16

46. Circle of Care: Clinical Issues in Jungian Therapy
Warren Steinberg (New York). ISBN 0-919123-47-3. 160 pp. $16

47. Jung Lexicon: A Primer of Terms & Concepts
Daryl Sharp (Toronto). ISBN 0-919123-48-1. 160 pp. $16

48. Body and Soul: The Other Side of Illness
Albert Kreinheder (Los Angeles). ISBN 0-919123-49-X. 112 pp. $16

49. Animus Aeternus: Exploring the Inner Masculine
Deldon Anne McNeely (Lynchburg, VA). ISBN 0-919123-50-3. 192 pp. $18

50. Castration and Male Rage: The Phallic Wound
Eugene Monick (Scranton, PA). ISBN 0-919123-51-1. 144 pp. $16

51. Saturday's Child: Encounters with the Dark Gods
Janet O. Dallett (Seal Harbor, WA). ISBN 0-919123-52-X. 128 pp. $16

52. The Secret Lore of Gardening: Patterns of Male Intimacy
Graham Jackson (Toronto). ISBN 0-919123-53-8. 160 pp. $16

53. The Refiner's Fire: Memoirs of a German Girlhood
Sigrid R. McPherson (Los Angeles). ISBN 0-919123-54-6. 208 pp. $18

54. Transformation of the God-Image: Jung's *Answer to Job*
Edward F. Edinger (Los Angeles). ISBN 0-919123-55-4. 144 pp. $16

55. Getting to Know You: The Inside Out of Relationship
Daryl Sharp (Toronto). ISBN 0-919123-56-2. 128 pp. $16

56. A Strategy for a Loss of Faith: Jung's Proposal
John P. Dourley (Ottawa). ISBN 0-919123-57-0. 144 pp. $16

57. Close Relationships: Family, Friendship, Marriage
Eleanor Bertine (New York). ISBN 0-919123-58-9. 160 pp. $16

58. Conscious Femininity: Interviews with Marion Woodman
Introduction by Marion Woodman (Toronto). ISBN 0-919123-59-7. 160 pp. $16

59. The Middle Passage: From Misery to Meaning in Midlife
James Hollis (Houston). ISBN 0-919123-60-0. 128 pp. $16

60. The Living Room Mysteries: Patterns of Male Intimacy, Book 2
Graham Jackson (Toronto). ISBN 0-919123-61-9. 144 pp. $16

61. Chicken Little: The Inside Story *(A Jungian Romance)*
Daryl Sharp (Toronto). ISBN 0-919123-62-7. 128 pp. $16

62. Coming To Age: The Croning Years and Late-Life Transformation
Jane R. Prétat (Providence, RI). ISBN 0-919123-63-5. 144 pp. $16

63. Under Saturn's Shadow: The Wounding and Healing of Men
James Hollis (Houston). ISBN 0-919123-64-3. 144 pp. $16

Discounts: any 3-5 books, 10%; 6-9 books, 20%; 10 or more, 25%
Add Postage/Handling: 1-2 books, $3; 3-4 books, $5; 5-9 books, $10; 10 or more, free

Write or phone for free Catalogue of **over 80 titles** and **Jung at Heart** newsletter

INNER CITY BOOKS

Box 1271, Station Q, Toronto, ON M4T 2P4, Canada   **(416) 927-0355**